MW00635492

An Introduction to
Collection Development for School Librarians

*Purchases of AASL Publications fund advocacy, leadership,
professional development, and standards initiatives for
school librarians nationally.*

❖

*ALA Editions purchases fund advocacy, awareness, and
accreditation programs for library professionals worldwide.*

MONA KERBY

An Introduction to

Collection Development for School Librarians

SECOND EDITION

American Association
of School Librarians
TRANSFORMING LEARNING

CHICAGO | 2019

MONA KERBY is professor and coordinator of graduate programs in school librarianship, instructional technology, and writing for children at McDaniel College in Maryland, where she holds the L. Stanley Bowlsbey Professor of Education and Graduate and Professional Studies Endowed Chair. She also writes award-winning books for children. See www.monakerby.com.

© 2019 by the American Library Association

Extensive effort has gone into ensuring the reliability of the information in this book; however, the publisher makes no warranty, express or implied, with respect to the material contained herein.

ISBN: 978-0-8389-1892-0 (paper)

Library of Congress Cataloging-in-Publication Data

Names: Kerby, Mona, author.
Title: An introduction to collection development for school librarians / Mona Kerby.
Other titles: Collection development for the school library media program
Description: Second edition. | Chicago : ALA Editions, 2019. | Includes bibliographical references and index.
Identifiers: LCCN 2019019817 | ISBN 9780838918920 (alk. paper)
Subjects: LCSH: School libraries—Collection development—United States. | Instructional materials centers—Collection development—United States.
Classification: LCC Z675.S3 K457 2019 | DDC 025.2/1878—dc23 LC record available at https://lccn.loc.gov/2019019817

Book design by Alejandra Diaz in the Utopia Std and Galano typefaces.

♾ This paper meets the requirements of ANSI/NISO Z39.48–1992 (Permanence of Paper).

Printed in the United States of America
23 22 21 20 19   5 4 3 2 1

CONTENTS

ACKNOWLEDGMENTS

Thanks to my McDaniel colleagues, my graduate students, Maryland school librarians, and AASL colleagues for their tips, ideas, and help in writing this book. You're the best!

Heather Beaton

Shari Blohm

Stephanie Book

Christine Carey

Shelby Conover

Carolyn Crabtree

April Dawkins

Gail Dickinson

Danielle DuPuis

Katie Florida

Jona French

Margaret Gaudino

Ariel Kifer

Dina Kropkowski

Cassandra Lopez

Jeanne Mayo

Thomas McNicholas

Rachel O'Connell

Mary Rasche

Jamie Rooney

Jamie Santoro

Jennifer Sturge

Dedra Van Gelder

Lynn Wilcox

Jen Yohe

INTRODUCTION
Ready to Roll Up Your Sleeves?

An Introduction to Collection Development for School Librarians is written for school librarians who are just beginning in the profession, for graduate candidates enrolled in collection development courses, and for practicing school librarians who want to improve their collections.

If you walk into a cluttered school library and start rolling up your sleeves, then you know you have the heart of a librarian. We like every aspect of organizing, figuring out who needs what, and buying new school library materials—especially with district money. Here's the essence of collection development boiled down to one question: What do I do with all this stuff?

This simple question doesn't have an easy answer. Managing a school library can be overwhelming. Some school librarians may handle collection development by not doing much of anything—except letting the dust collect. Okay, so I'm trying to be funny about your unexpected but everlasting nemesis—dust.

But let me get back to the point. Not having a collection development plan is wrong. We live in this digital age in which information multiplies at a dizzying rate. Our learners need access to quality materials. Yet too many school libraries are filled with dusty, outdated, and inaccurate materials. To look at these collections is nothing short of heartbreaking. Our learners deserve better.

The aging collections aren't entirely our fault. After the Russians launched Sputnik in 1957, the U.S. government poured money into school libraries, and for decades, libraries benefited from government funding. But over the past four decades, school library budgets have been slashed by politicians and administrators. Although school librarians may not be to blame, we're the ones our learners depend on. For our learners to thrive in a digital age, they must have access to quality materials and know how to use them. We cannot disappoint our learners; the consequences are too dire—for them, for our country, and for the world.

In 2006 the American Association of School Librarians (AASL) published my book on collection development. It stayed in print for twelve years, which was a pretty good run, but now it is time for a new edition with substantial revisions.

This new edition addresses collection development using AASL's *National School Library Standards for Learners, School Librarians, and School Libraries.* Other changes involve the inclusion of digital materials in building a school library collection. Databases and e-books are a reality in today's school libraries, and you'll want to know how to purchase them. In the old days, we collected circulation data by hand, but now your automated circulation systems can provide this information within minutes, and we'll explore the available options. And, though some professional selection sources are still available in print, we'll identify what is available digitally. In this edition, chapter 8 discusses the ways to showcase your collection. Building a quality collection is no longer enough; you must ensure that learners actively use and engage with the materials.

This edition also reflects the latest preparation standards that guide coursework in nationally recognized graduate school librarianship programs. Written by the American Library Association (ALA) and AASL, the *Standards for Initial Preparation of School Librarians* are approved by the Council for the Accreditation of Educator Preparation (CAEP). For our purposes, I am only referring to the ALA/AASL/CAEP preparation standards that concern collection development (ALA/AASL/CAEP, forthcoming).

What remains the same in this edition is my approach and writing voice. There is a great textbook on collection development, and I use it in my graduate course, but the textbook is 330 pages long. The textbook tells you everything, sometimes more than you want to know. I believe in being succinct, practical, and to the point. When you're busy—and you are if you're in graduate school and a practicing school librarian—you don't have time to wade through an excess of information.

You need to focus on the essentials and use your time wisely. I will help. I've read our professional literature on collection development, but in this book, I'm not regurgitating everything. Instead, I'm giving you the highlights. You'll find summaries, charts, examples, and tips from practicing school librarians. After reading this book, you will be able to create an outstanding school library collection by (1) analyzing curriculum and user needs; (2) using policies and procedures to evaluate, weed, and build a collection; and (3) engaging your learners in actively using the collection. In short, I'll give you the key information you need to ensure your success.

I'll be writing in an informal tone, using contractions and the pronoun *you,* because I am talking to you. I'll use the pronoun *she* for consistency. I am not including URL links because they can change overnight. Instead, I'll give you the full title of a resource, or I'll provide a strong search phrase you can use in your search engine.

A quick explanation about vocabulary: I'll use the common language found in the *National School Library Standards*. The term *learners* will indicate everyone in the building. If I need to indicate that I am referring only to students, I'll use the term *student learners.* For teachers, I'll say *classroom educators.* I'll use the terms *school librarian* and *school library,* so you know I'm not referring to other librarians and libraries. Our ALA/AASL/CAEP preparation standards use the word *candidates* for adult students in graduate programs to differentiate them from preK–12 learners. Whenever I mention my graduate students, I'll use the term *candidates.* I'll use the term *school library handbook,* even though more than likely the information is not on paper but is located on your district's portal.

I hope you'll find my writing voice plain-speaking, sometimes opinionated, and frequently funny. I'll let you know when I'm spouting off my opinion, especially when it differs from an AASL official position. I'll use the phrase *Kerby opinion alert.* You should know right now you can ignore my opinion.

One time my husband muttered, "I don't know why you ever ask for my opinion because you never do what I say." And I replied, "Yes, but your opinion helped me make up my own mind." In this book, I'm giving you a touchstone to make your own decisions.

In fact, I'm expecting you to participate in this learning journey. At the end of each chapter, you'll find a "Your Turn" section in which you jot down the ideas that resonated with you and in which you craft your plan of action for what needs to be done in your school library.

So, who am I? And why should you take this learning journey with me? I grew up in Texas, and I became a kindergarten teacher in the Arlington (Texas) Independent School District. I never thought of being a school librarian until I happened to see a flyer on the teachers' lounge bulletin board. The flyer changed everything. I became the school librarian at Little Elementary in Arlington at the same time that I went to graduate school at Texas Woman's University to earn my MLS and then eventually my PhD. I fell in love with school librarianship. After my doctorate, I stayed for years at Little School and started writing books for children.

After a couple of decades, I happened to see an advertisement for an assistant professor in school librarianship. In Maryland. My husband, our dog, and I up and moved. We'd never lived anywhere but Texas. And what did we discover? We love Maryland.

I made my second career at McDaniel College in Westminster, Maryland, where I coordinate three graduate programs in school librarianship, in learning technologies, and in writing for children. I am honored to hold the L. Stanley Bowlsbey Professor of Education and Graduate and Professional Studies Endowed Chair; I've been awarded the Outstanding Teacher of the Year Award. I am active in AASL; I serve as an auditor for university programs seeking national recognition on the ALA/AASL/CAEP preparation program standards. And I've written about collection development for decades.

Back at Little School where I was the library teacher, whenever we had a musical performance, all our students received the same pattern and fabric for their costumes, but on the night of the performance, all those costumes looked different, unique. Seamstresses don't sew the same.

That is exactly what will be happening here. We're following the same pattern, but the outcomes will not be identical. You are designing for your own school communities.

Here's our mission. We will practice the art of collection development. I'll make the simplest and clearest pattern I can. You weave a beautiful design. Ready? Roll up your sleeves, and let's go to work.

What Do I Do First?

When you interviewed for your new position, you may not have seen the school library. One of my graduate candidates was hired a week before school started while she was in another state, and only when she walked into the school library did she realize why the district was so quick to hire her while she wasn't there—the books were molding, and the dehumidifiers couldn't work fast enough. Even in the best of positions, when school begins, expect to feel a touch of panic.

WHAT DO I DO ON THE FIRST DAY?

Take a deep breath and smile. When you feel stressed, remember you're not a brain surgeon. If you're a little slow, no one will code. I answered most questions with "I don't know, but I'll let you know when I find out."

—Jeanne Mayo, School Librarian, Liberty High School, Carroll County Public Schools, Maryland

---

To be entirely candid, you may be overwhelmed. This happens for several reasons. Even though you no doubt read the job expectations, if you're a classroom educator, you probably thought the school librarian's job was easier than yours. After all, school librarians just spend their time reading and checking out books, right? When beginning school librarians express shock at all their new responsibilities, experienced school librarians laugh. But we laugh because we remember that same surprise. Suddenly, you're responsible for thousands of materials and hundreds of learners, and you need to know them all. You've got all sorts of multiple passwords and logins to remember. If you're in an elementary school, you've got at least six different lesson plans to write—for grades you've never taught before. Other educators and learners keep coming in, interrupting your concentration, and wanting something—immediately. I can remember wishing for a bigger brain. I started taking vitamins.

You might inherit a clean, organized, and pristine school library, but don't count on it. Classroom carts and equipment may have been stored in the school library over the summer, and you'll need to get those checked out to classroom educators and moved back to the classrooms. Your mailbox will be piled with catalogs and magazines to sort. You might have a new shipment of books. You've got bulletin boards to make, lessons to plan, and staff to meet. What do you do first?

When you were a classroom educator, only thirty learners might talk about you at suppertime. In the school library classroom where you teach everyone, you might be the topic of conversation at hundreds of supper tables. You get one chance to make a first impression. Don't blow it. No pressure.

IF YOU FEED THEM, THEY WILL COME

Offer an early morning meet and greet to introduce yourself. A small investment in bagels will pay back tenfold. It's hard to say no to someone, once you've broken bread with them.

—Cassandra Lopez, Northfield Elementary School Librarian,
Howard County Public Schools, Maryland

Twelve Tasks for the First Weeks of School

Here is a list of tasks to tackle. Prioritize them.

1. *Learn to use the circulation system.* Add all new users to the system. If classroom equipment is housed in the school library, check out the items and move them to the classrooms. Getting rid of this clutter will make you feel better.
2. *Meet the classroom educators.* Before school starts, send a short, friendly personal e-mail to every educator. By writing one e-mail at a time, you're learning names and who teaches what. In the e-mail, ask what pressing needs the educator has that you might help with. Ask the lead grade-level educators for some suggested times that you might stop by to meet their team. Stop by each classroom and

briefly introduce yourself. Be friendly and quick. Busy educators appreciate quick conversations.

3. *Find your district school library handbook and read it.* For some reason, you'll think you're too busy, but this is where you'll find the answers to most of your questions. Don't read every word, but do spend time scanning topics. You'll find information about:

    a. Running statistical reports
    b. Information technology resources
    c. Internet use
    d. Budget and ordering procedures
    e. Processing/barcodes
    f. Guidelines for weeding school library materials
    g. Discarding weeded materials
    h. Donations and gifts
    i. Job descriptions
    j. Circulation procedures, including patron privileges and fines
    k. Selection criteria and professional selection sources
    l. Policies approved by the school board
    m. Mission and vision statements
    n. ALA policies, procedures, and statements

    All district school library handbooks will have this information because they reflect the wording and ideals of ALA and AASL. If your district doesn't provide you with a current handbook, then go straight to the ALA website. Use this cookie trail—ALA > Tools, Publications & Resources > Challenge Support > Selection & Reconsideration Policy Toolkit—so you can read "Selection & Reconsideration Policy Toolkit for Public, School, & Academic Libraries." This inspiring and easy-to-read document was updated and approved in January 2018 (ALA 2018).

4. *Plan your lessons.* Those first few weeks of lessons need to be simple and, most especially, memorable. Simple because you will be short on time. Memorable because your learners need to go back to their classrooms and homes, enthusiastically explaining what they learned in the school library and how much fun they had. All learners must check out books and materials the first week. Teach lessons that are simple, memorable, and positive.

5. *Locate popular sections of the school library.* If you're an elementary school librarian, you will likely have forty-five-minute classes. You won't have time to individually help every learner to find a book by using the Online Public Access Catalog (OPAC). Before classes start, learn the locations of these sections—dinosaurs, animals, pets, jokes, sports, world records, graphic novels, and books by popular authors.

6. *Learn the logins for the OPAC and databases.* Make yourself reminder notes and keep this information handy.
7. *Prepare bulletin boards and decorate the school library.* This task can take days, so before you start, decide how much time you're going to give to this project. Find a volunteer who might help.
8. *Organize, declutter, and dust.* As the school library educator, your classroom is observed by everyone all the time. A neat and tidy school library indicates—without you ever opening your mouth—that you're organized, that books and learning are important, and that you're here to help. Create a book hospital for replacing torn covers and mending pages and spines. Book repair needs to be a weekly job, and you need to purchase the tape and covers from a library company. Early on, get a stash of dustrags, spray cleaner, and heavy-duty opaque trash bags. Don't use see-through bags. Just so you know, people look at your school library trash.
9. *Prepare a school library grade book.* Call roll for each class and practice names. Within the first six weeks, you must know everyone's name. Period. This one action makes a powerful impact. It tells your community one thing—you care.
10. *Ask to do five-minute workshops at educators' meetings throughout the year.* Show technology tools that are useful and time-saving. Each summer at ALA's Annual Conference, AASL announces the yearly lists of Best Apps and Best Websites for Teaching & Learning. Bookmark this web page.
11. *Buy a new outfit.* My grandmother taught during the Depression, and money was always tight. She didn't buy many new dresses, but when she did, she would grin and say, "Why, this isn't for me. This dress is for the children." Student learners stare at you and notice everything. In fact, because you want to look professional and tidy, you may want to buy several outfits. This bullet point gives you official professional permission to spend some money on yourself. You're welcome.
12. *Tasks for home.* You'll need six weeks to adjust to your new job. Go easy on yourself. Still, know you'll be arriving early and staying late, so stock up on frozen dinners and underwear—you may not have much time to cook or wash.

Suggestions from School Library Supervisors

I have the highest respect for school library supervisors. Not only do they have practical experience from their years of being school librarians, but also they have wisdom based on their experience of working with district personnel and community leaders. The following suggestions from outstanding school library supervisors help you focus on what to do.

Have One Goal

Make a cheat sheet that includes the important people you need to know with their phone numbers and e-mail addresses, school codes, links to resources, key logins, and deadlines. This is a job you grow in. Do not try to change or do everything at once. Get to know your learners. Pick one or two things to work on the first year. No one accomplishes twelve goals at a time. Pick the thing that irritates you the most or the thing that will give you a noticeable benefit. As for specific actionable items, get your first week's lessons planned. Determine the circulation policies and share the information with the school community.

—Dedra Van Gelder, Content Specialist—Library Media,
Charles County Public Schools, Maryland

Build Positive Relationships

New school librarians tend to get hung up on the enormity of the job and then gravitate to cosmetic things such as making bulletin boards and organizing shelves. In my opinion, they should learn the curriculum and build positive relationships with the staff, the student learners, and the community. Curriculum and relationships will guide school librarians through everything else that occurs or needs to be done.

—Jona French, Supervisor of Library Media and Instructional Technology,
Washington County Public Schools, Maryland

Teach

First and foremost, the school librarian is an educator. Prepare a strong first lesson and allow learners to check out books the first week. Don't tell learners they can't check out books for several weeks. Be welcoming. Become a part of the school culture.

—Jennifer Sturge, Specialist for School Libraries,
Calvert County Public Schools, Maryland

Communicate

You'll have so many questions! You'll want to ask about the opening week schedule and your responsibilities, how the school library might be scheduled before and after school, and the amount of your budget, if it even exists. Communication is essential to your success.

1. Apply your best listening skills, and be patient and kind. Your opinions will be heard more readily if you appear to be working as a team member.

2. Find volunteers, including previous ones and any who need to be vetted. Better to have them on call rather than being overwhelmed a month into school.
3. Reach out to the extended community to introduce yourself digitally and in person, including at the local public library.
4. Make a friend or two on the faculty and support them. Others will notice and want your help as well.
5. Communicate with your central office if requests seem out of line; ask for a mentor or "buddy" librarian in the district.

—Shari Blohm, EdS, Instructional Supervisor, Office of Library Media Services, Prince George's County Public Schools, Maryland

---

I still remember my first weeks as the Little School librarian. I didn't know any of the educators or the learners. In those years, I was still shy, and the classroom educators scared me. I knew how to teach kindergarten, but when I taught the sixth graders, my voice shook. On one lonely afternoon after most of the other educators had left, and I was still working—on boring tasks that had never occurred to me school librarians even did—I was missing my old kindergarten classroom.

But I got over it. Sure, I was still overwhelmed. But there I was—surrounded by ten thousand books just waiting to be read and cherished. Instead of thirty kindergarteners, I now had some six hundred kids who were already smiling at me. They were making me laugh with the funny things they said. By the end of the second six-week marking period, I knew one thing for sure.

I had the best job in the world.

YOUR TURN

Chapter 1—What Do I Do First?

In this chapter, what were the most important ideas that surprised or resonated with you?

_____

_____

_____

According to the *National School Library Standards,* a school librarian is a leader, an instructional partner, a teacher, an information specialist, and a program administrator. Identify where you are strong and where you need to learn. Identify one or two ways to demonstrate each role.

_____

_____

_____

List everything you want to do in this job for the day, for the week, for the year, for the decade. Messy is fine. Just get it down.

_____

_____

_____

Select three immediate tasks. Prepare a statement for each item, describing what you are going to do in a measurable way. Identify the resources (AASL, district level, people) you need in order to accomplish each task. State how much time you can allot to each.

_____

_____

_____

Chapter 1 worksheet supporting *An Introduction to Collection Development for School Librarians* by Mona Kerby, © 2019 American Library Association.

 For a one-page, printable version of this worksheet, go to **alaeditions.org/webextras.**

What Should I Learn Next?

Even though I haven't been an elementary school librarian for years, I have a recurring nightmare. I've been moved to a new school library where the learners and other educators keep asking me for help, and I keep circling the shelves, but I don't have the books I need. I always wake up frustrated. No telling what a psychoanalyst would say, but let's not digress. Here's my point. There are plenty of school librarians who don't buy quality materials, and their collection development plans do not meet learner needs.

Beginners make mistakes, and I know because I made them. Once, I purchased a set of nonfiction books because they were on sale, and the titles matched some of the curriculum. Well, those books arrived. They were bound in the same color, the writing was boring, and the page layout was terrible. My Little School student learners wouldn't touch them.

In Maryland, there are several friendly salespersons who regularly stop by uninvited at school libraries. They have a suitcase of nonfiction books with titles that exactly meet the state curriculum. What's more, the books are on sale. The deal looks too good to be true.

It is.

Those publishing companies are small. The books weren't vetted as they were being written and edited. Professional reviewers didn't recommend most of the titles. I've seen those books, just sitting on Maryland school library shelves. Untouched. Money wasted.

Quicker than you expect, you will have to prepare a materials order. To do this successfully, you must (1) know your standards, (2) know your learners, (3) know the curriculum, and (4) identify your selection criteria. These four responsibilities not only help you prepare successful orders; your accomplishment of them ensures that you are successful in every aspect of school librarianship.

Step 1: Know Your Standards

In the old days, school librarians were successful if they just built a collection. Today, learners must *use* the school library collection. The materials you buy must provide learners with multiple opportunities to meet AASL's *National School Library Standards for Learners, School Librarians, and School Libraries.* Your purchases and your professional activities are informed by the four Domains—A. Think, B. Create, C. Share, and D. Grow—and by the six Shared Foundations—I. Inquire, II. Include, III. Collaborate, IV. Curate, V. Explore, and VI. Engage (figure 2.1). Learners must have educational opportunities for each, and this means your collection must have appropriate materials.

National School Library Standards: AASL Standards Framework for School Libraries

The frameworks for each of the six Shared Foundations in the *National School Library Standards* are great; we can easily see the expectations for learners, school librarians, and school libraries and how the three connect. In this introduction to collection development, let's focus on the relevant Alignments found in the *AASL Standards Framework for School Libraries.*

For our purposes, I've selected twelve School Library Domains and Alignments that pertain to collection development. In figure 2.2 the most important ideas within each of the Alignments listed are in boldface. In this book, I'll show you strategies to help meet these standards (AASL 2018, 59–64).

Fundamental to collection development are two Alignments that we will repeatedly discuss. First, we must provide "access to resources, information, ideas, and technology for **all learners in the school community**" (AASL 2018, School Library I.B.1.). This statement seems obvious, doesn't it? But many beginning school librarians can't articulate who their learners are. School librarians might mention autistic learners or special needs classes, but many librarians are unable to effectively articulate the characteristics of all learners.

Second, we are to establish and maintain "a collection of reading and information **materials in formats that support the diverse developmental, cultural, social, and linguistic needs of the range of learners and their communities**" (AASL 2018, School Library II.B.1.). This statement clearly identifies the characteristics of your learners that you need to know. Personalizing the collection and the instruction elevates learners' connection to the content; the learning becomes authentic; and this connection ensures that the collection will indeed be used.

FIGURE 2.1

Flowchart for *AASL Standards Integrated Framework*

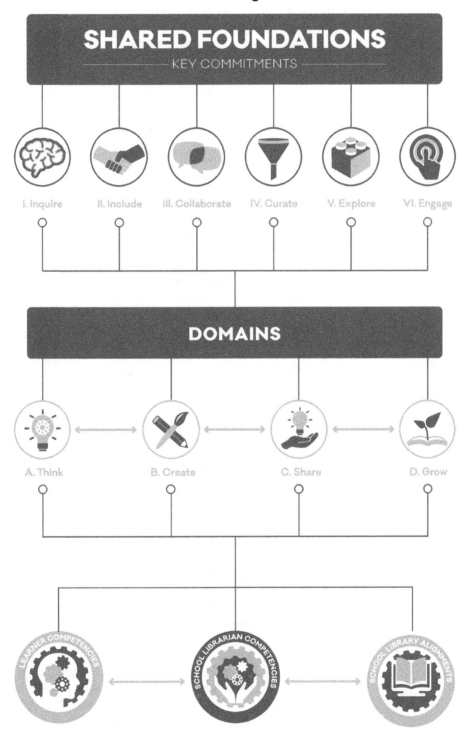

Source: Excerpted from the AASL *National School Library Standards for Learners, School Librarians, and School Libraries*, standards.aasl.org, © 2018 American Library Association.

FIGURE 2.2

National School Library Standards: School Library Domains and Alignments for Collection Development

Shared Foundations	School Library Domains and Alignments
I. Inquire	**B. CREATE:** The school library enables generation of new knowledge by: • I.B.1. Providing experiences with and **access to resources, information, ideas, and technology for all learners** in the school community.
II. Include	**A. THINK:** The school library supports balanced perspectives through resources and learning opportunities by: • II.A.3. Providing a **comprehensive variety** of resources. **B. CREATE:** The school library represents all members and their place in a global learning community by: • II.B.1. Establishing and maintaining a collection of reading and information **materials in formats that support the diverse developmental, cultural, social, and linguistic needs of the range of learners and their communities.** **C. SHARE:** The school library facilitates opportunities to experience diverse ideas by: • II.C.2. Promoting the use of **high-quality and high-interest literature in formats that reflect the diverse developmental, cultural, social, and linguistic needs of all learners** and their communities. • II.C.3. Constructing a learning environment that fosters the sharing of **a wide range of viewpoints and ideas**. **D. GROW:** The school library builds empathy and equity within the global learning community by: • II.D.1. Ensuring that all learning needs are met through access to information and ideas located in **a diverse collection of sufficient size** for the learner population and supported by reliable hardware and software.
III. Collaborate	**A. THINK:** The school library facilitates opportunities to integrate collaborative and shared learning by: • III.A.2. Leading inquiry-based learning opportunities that **enhance the information, media, visual, and technical literacies** of all members of the school community.
IV. Curate	**A. THINK:** The school library provides problem-based learning experiences and environments by: • IV.A.2. Adopting a dynamic **collection-development plan** to ensure that adequate resources **reflect current and in-depth knowledge**. **B. CREATE:** The school library promotes selection of appropriate resources and tools for information use by: • IV.B.3. Employing a **dynamic collection policy that includes selection and retention criteria for all materials** within the collection. **D. GROW:** The school library engages the learning community in exploring resources by: • IV.D.2. **Maintaining a collection of sufficient breadth and currency to be pertinent to the school's program of studies.**
V. Explore	**A. THINK:** The school library supports learners' personal curiosity by: • V.A.2. Fostering opportunities for learners to demonstrate personal curiosity and creation of knowledge through **engaging with a wide variety of resources and technology**.
VI. Engage	**D. GROW:** The school library supports individual responsibility for information use by: • VI.D.2. Providing an engaging learning environment that **supports innovative and ethical use of information and information technologies**.

Source: Excerpted from the AASL *National School Library Standards for Learners, School Librarians, and School Libraries*, standards.aasl.org, © 2018 American Library Association.

FIGURE 2.3

Learners Experience School Librarians' Roles through Domains

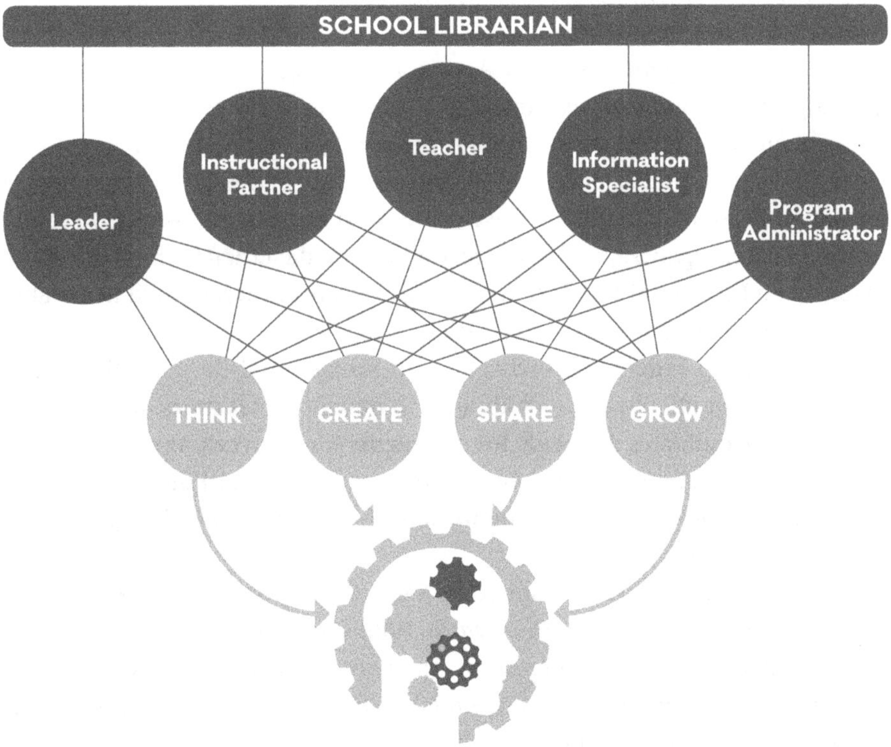

Source: Excerpted from the AASL *National School Library Standards for Learners, School Librarians, and School Libraries*, standards.aasl.org, © 2018 American Library Association.

In a very real way, you're a living example of the *National School Library Standards* (figure 2.3). You're a leader, an instructional partner, a teacher, an information specialist, and a program administrator (AASL 2018, 14–16). You're ensuring that learners will think, create, share, and grow by using the six Shared Foundations.

ALA/AASL/CAEP Standards for Initial Preparation of School Librarians

As I mentioned earlier, the ALA/AASL/CAEP preparation standards guide the coursework in nationally recognized graduate school librarianship programs. If you are a graduate school librarianship professor or a graduate candidate in an ALA/AASL/CAEP-recognized university or program, then your assignments are designed to meet these preparation standards. Three of the five preparation standards reflect collection development.

In Standard 1: The Learner and Learning, candidates demonstrate **learner development, diversity, and differences of their learners**. In Component 1.4 Learning Environments, candidates provide a learning environment that supports the **curation and creation** of knowledge.

In Standard 4: Organization and Access, candidates demonstrate their ability to develop, curate, organize, and manage a collection of resources to the meet the **diverse needs and interests** of a global society. In Component 4.1 Access, candidates provide equitable **access to resources** and services. In Component 4.2 Information Resources, candidates use **evaluation criteria and selection tools to develop, curate, organize, and manage a collection designed to meet the diverse curricular and personal needs of the learning community**. Candidates evaluate and select information resources in a variety of formats.

In Standard 5: Leadership, Advocacy, and Professional Responsibility, candidates advocate for effective school libraries to benefit **all learners.** In Component 5.3 Advocacy, candidates **advocate for all learners, resources, services, policies, procedures**, and school libraries. In Component 5.4 Ethical Practice, candidates model and promote the **ethical practices** of the library profession (ALA/AASL/CAEP, forthcoming).

You will immediately see how the ALA/AASL/CAEP preparation standards support the *National School Library Standards.* Both sets of standards ensure that you provide for all learner needs and provide open access to all materials, that you use selection criteria and model our professional ethical practices, and that you create a learning environment that supports the creation of knowledge.

If you are currently in graduate school, you will most likely have assignments related to identifying the learners, curriculum, and selection criteria because these assignments will document that you have met ALA/AASL/CAEP Standards 1 and 4.

Step 2: Know Your Learners

So who are the learners at your school? Begin by collecting the available data—test scores, census records, or information that is freely available on the district website. Don't wallow in excessive data; collect just what you need to give you an accurate snapshot of the community. Focus on the "diverse developmental, cultural, social, and linguistic needs of the range of learners" (AASL 2018, School Library II.B.1.).

Support this data collection by observing, listening, and asking questions. Which classroom educators use the school library, and what kinds of assignments do they give? What are the educators' instructional styles? What are the subjects that need strong school library support? Identify the various learning abilities of the student learners. What kinds of materials should you buy for their reading pleasure?

Gathering Information about Learners

Use the following bulleted lists as guides when collecting data about learners.

- The Community
  - The makeup of the community
  - Socioeconomic status
  - Cultural backgrounds
  - Languages spoken and read
  - Changes in demographics in the past five years
  - Student mobility
  - Homes with computer access
  - Access to public library service

- The School
  - Number of student learners and classroom educators
  - Trends in test scores
  - Academic achievement scores
  - Subject areas in which learners are doing poorly
  - Special school programs (academic, technical, etc.)
  - Access to the school library (whole classes, groups, individuals)
  - Primary users and nonusers of the school library
  - Recreational information needs
  - Personal information needs
  - Parental involvement
  - Mission statement of school

Using the data you have collected, craft a reflective analysis that comprehensively identifies and explains all learner needs. What does the collected information tell you about all the learners? What diversity should be addressed? What types of materials would you expect in this collection? Does the entire population appear to be adequately served by the school library collection? What materials do learners need in order to have opportunities to think, create, share, grow, and learn? What immediate purchases should be made?

Elementary School Learner Analysis

The following elementary school learner analysis was created by one of my graduate candidates. (Just so you know, she earned an A on the assignment.) But as I've been writing this chapter, I've been wondering how I might help my future candidates to craft an even deeper and more comprehensive analysis. The key wording in II.B.1. and II.C.2. regarding the "diverse developmental, cultural, social, and linguistic needs" of the range of learners should help with this deeper analysis. What else do you need to know about your community?

Cannon Road Elementary School User Analysis (2017)
Rachel O'Connell

- The makeup of the community:
  - 35.5 percent African American
  - 46 percent Hispanic
  - 5 percent White
  - 10 percent Asian
  - 3.5 percent Other/Mixed

- Socioeconomic status:
  - 67 percent FARMS (free and reduced meal student)

- Cultural backgrounds:
  - Forty-eight of the sixty-two ESOL (English for speakers of other languages) students were born in the United States.
  - Sixteen student learners were born outside the United States: El Salvador (four), Sierra Leone (two), Honduras (two), Haiti (two). One student each is from Ethiopia, Cote D'Ivoire, Congo, Chad, Bangladesh, and the Philippines.

- Languages spoken and read:
  - Spanish (84 percent), French, Creole/Pidgin/French, Chinese, Vietnamese, Tagalog, Bengali, and Russian

- Changes in demographics in the past five years:
  - Asian and Black have remained about the same
  - White down, Hispanic up significantly

- Student mobility: 15 percent
- Homes with computer access: ~33 percent
- Access to public library service: Public library is within five miles of neighborhood

The School

- Numbers of student learners and educators: 425 student learners, 40 professional staff

- Academic achievement scores:
  - 64 percent of K–2nd graders met the Montgomery County (Maryland) Public Schools (MCPS) benchmark on math test
  - 38 percent of 3rd–5th graders met the MCPS benchmark on math test
  - 60 percent of K–2nd graders met the MCPS benchmark on reading test
  - 48 percent of 3rd–5th graders met MCPS benchmark on reading test

- Subject areas in which student learners are doing poorly: math, reading
- Special school programs (academic, technical, etc.):
    - Augmentative and Alternative Communication (AAC) program
    - Homeschool model of inclusion
    - Learning and Academic Disabilities (LAD) program
    - Positive Behavioral Interventions and Supports (PBIS)

- Recreational information needs:
    - Animal books, especially hamsters, guinea pigs, dogs, and cats
    - Sports biographies
    - Drawing books
    - Books in Spanish/English
    - Occasional requests for origami, magic tricks, science experiments, rocks, and wars

- Personal information needs:
    - Books on "my country" (the country the learner is from)
    - Some requests for books on religion and on babies, especially when a new sibling is expected

- Parental involvement:
    - Small group of involved parents
    - 50 percent of families join the PTA

SCHOOL ANALYSIS

The elementary school, located in Silver Spring, Maryland, opened in 1967. For the first twenty-five to thirty years, the school was predominantly White and middle class, and the learners lived in the surrounding neighborhood. In the 1990s, learners from an apartment complex about ten minutes away were redistricted to Cannon Road. Many houses in the neighborhood are now occupied by multiple generations of immigrant families. The numbers of African American and Hispanic learners have increased dramatically. Currently, the collection doesn't adequately reflect the school's diversity, although we do have some materials written in Spanish, which is the largest demographic. In the future, the school librarian will purchase books on countries, biographies of women scientists and people of color, and novels in which the characters represent a wider diversity of backgrounds. I hope the school librarian will purchase books on sports, drawing, animals, and graphic novels because these are popular topics.

—Rachel O'Connell, School Library Media Specialist, William Tyler Page Elementary School, Montgomery County Public Schools, Maryland

CHECKLIST FOR PREPARING THE CURRICULUM CHART

Content

1. Does the chart reflect the district curriculum at the elementary, middle, or high school level?
2. Do the selected subjects help the school librarian purchase suitable materials to meet the needs of the curriculum and learners? Is the chart richer in social studies and science topics?
3. Is the chart of use to educators when planning schoolwide curriculum and to parents in supporting students' learning?
4. Has the chart been prepared for a specific school?
5. Does the chart avoid educational jargon?
6. Are the subjects listed briefly, and do they make sense?
7. Does the most important word appear first?
8. Are vague and unnecessary topics deleted—such as "Language Experience" or "Problem Solving"?
9. Do the phrases begin the same—with noun or verb?
10. Do the selected phrases allow them to be linked to grade-level-appropriate Internet sites?

Aesthetics

1. Is the overall design pleasing and professional, with appropriately sized fonts and with plenty of white space?
2. Does the creator include her name, the date of revision (month/day/year), and source of the information in a small font? Is the chart one page or two pages at most (8½ by 11)?
3. Is the chart in a format that is easily distributed via print, e-mail, and the web?

Step 3: Know the Curriculum

In my first year as a school librarian, a third-grade educator asked if we had enough books on planets for her learners to do research. I stood there dumbfounded. Oh. We study planets in third grade? Maybe I should know what all the grades study. Duh.

Looking back, I don't know how I missed that in graduate school. I'm sure curriculum was mentioned. But I had no idea what subjects were covered. I was a classroom educator, but I only knew the curriculum for my grade, not for the entire school.

Well, this mistake will not happen to you because the School Library Alignment IV.D.2. states that you need to maintain a collection of breadth and currency pertinent to the school's studies. We'll tackle breadth and currency in later chapters, but for now, focus on the school curriculum.

I wish I could tell you that you'll find a clear and simple curriculum chart that highlights the key topics taught in your district. But you won't. The curriculum guides are filled with excessive amounts of vague and ambiguous educational jargon. You will have to search for the essential kernels of the topics taught and delete the chaff.

You'll spend more time than you expect, studying the confusing curriculum, talking to the classroom educators, and polishing the wording in the chart so the topics make sense. But, oh, the time is well spent. Although the primary reason you are making the chart is for you to have an easy-to-read buying guide for selecting materials, the chart will help with your collaborative lessons with other educators. Because the chart looks professional, your principal may share it with the faculty and parents/guardians. Surprisingly, many educators don't know what their colleagues teach. Parents eager to help their children with school will have a terrific resource. When you share the school curriculum in a one-page, professionally formatted chart, people will think you're smart. And dedicated. That's the reputation you want. Post the chart everywhere, including the school library website.

Although the chart will reflect the district or state curriculum, tailor it to your own building. Ask one or two educators in each grade level and subject area to look over your topics and see if you've captured everything. Don't send an e-mail—educators may not answer; they're busy. Bring the chart with you to lunch or chat in the hall with the other educators for a few minutes. The discussion won't take long. Mention that you have money to spend on materials. The educators will help.

Find out how long educators plan to spend on a topic and how they plan to teach the topic. That information will give you an idea of how many items you need. If student learners do group projects, you'll need fewer items than when learners do individual research. Ask how long the unit lasts. For a two-week research unit, you'll want more books than for a one-day lesson. Ask when the unit is taught; you'll know what to place on the next order.

FIGURE 2.4

Piney Ridge Elementary School Curriculum

	English Language Arts	Social Studies	Science
Kindergarten	• Characters • Setting • Realistic fiction • Fantasy • Fables	• U.S. Flag/Pledge of Allegiance • Martin Luther King Jr. • Statue of Liberty • George Washington • Globes/maps • Landforms/ water	• Butterfly life cycle • Frog life cycle • Forces • Seasons • Temperature • Severe weather
1st Grade	• Key details • Text features • Fantasy • Realistic fiction • How-to writing	• Bald eagle • Government holidays • Map symbols • Continents • Economic wants/needs • Goods/services	• Moon • Seeds • Plant parts • Plant/animal heredity • Animal/plant habitats • Pollination
2nd Grade	• Topic • Text features • Fables • Folktales • Opinion writing	• U.S. symbols • Rosa Parks • Pollution • Types of communities • Natural/capital/human resources	• Water properties • Landforms • Erosion • Heating/cooling • Sound/light • Reflections
3rd Grade	• Character traits • Main idea • Fables • Myths • Research writing	• Mass production • Carroll County • Migration • Mexico/China • U.S. regions	• Weather • Climate • Natural disasters • Plant/animal cycles • Matter
4th Grade	• Theme • Point of view • Dramas • Poetry • Research writing	• Maryland geography • Revolutionary War • War of 1812 • Civil War • Maryland government • Chesapeake Bay conflict/ environmental changes	• Chesapeake Bay biodiversity • Speed • Energy transfer • Energy types • Waves • Erosion
5th Grade	• Theme • Point of view • Quoting text • Poetry • Novels	• Early settlements • Colonial America • Boston Massacre • Boston Tea Party • Revolutionary War • Great Compromise • Gov't branches	• Plant/animal adaptations • Native/invasive plants • Fossils • Water cycle • Earth rotation • Gravity

Art	
K–2nd Grade	**3rd Grade–5th Grade**
• Line • Form • Shape • Texture	• Monumental sculpture • Print-making • Clay • Sewing

Mathematics	Music	Health	
• Whole numbers • 2-D shapes • 3-D shapes	• Rhythm • Steady beat • Fast/slow tempo • High/low pitch	• Feelings/behavior • Bullying/teasing • Medicine safety • Healthy foods	Kindergarten
• +/- with 20 • Multiples of 10 • Measurement • Geometric shapes	• Quarter note • Quarter rest • Pitch matching	• Decision making • Personal space/boundaries • Nicotine/tobacco • Germs	1st Grade
• Money • +/- of 2 and 3 digits • Measure length • 2-D shapes	• Strong/weak beat • Half note • Half rest • Verse/refrain	• Meaning of emotions • Healthy peer relationships • Stress management • Food safety	2nd Grade
• x/÷ • Area • Time • Fractions	• =/≠ beat • Whole note • Whole rest • Pentatonic scale	• Verbal/nonverbal communication • Empathy/compassion • Body image • Caffeine	3rd Grade
• +/- of multiple digits • x/÷ up to 4 digits • Powers of 10 • Area/perimeter	• Eighth/sixteenth note • Treble clef • Countermelody • Soprano/alto	• Wellness factors • Vaping • Media influence • Nutritious/nonnutritious beverages	4th Grade
• Quadrilaterals • Decimals +/-/x/÷ • Fractions +/-/x/÷ • Coordinate planes	• Syncopation • Downbeat/upbeat • Major/minor scales	• Coping with stress • Marijuana • Peer pressure • Balanced meal planning	5th Grade

Physical Education

• Basketball	• Floor hockey	• Lacrosse	• Tennis
• Bowling	• Gymnastics	• Rope climbing	• Throwing/catching
• Dance	• Jump rope	• Soccer	• Volleyball

Source: Jen Yohe, Teacher, Piney Ridge Elementary School, Carroll County Public Schools, Maryland

FIGURE 2.5

South Hagerstown High School Curriculum At-A-Glance

	Science	Social Studies	Language Arts	Math
9th Grade	**Biology** • Cycles of Life • Cells and Organisms • Molecular Structure and Function • Genetics • Heredity • Environmental and Social Concerns	**US History II** • Industrialization • US Imperialism • Great Depression • World War I and II • The Roaring 20s • Cold War • The Red Scare • 1960s and Vietnam • Terrorism	**English 9** • Fiction • Literary Nonfiction • Research Skills • Thesis Development • Editing and Revising • Grammar and Vocabulary	**Algebra 1 and 2** • Systems of Equations • Slopes and Intercepts • Polynomial and Relational Functions • Graphing
10th Grade	**Chemistry** • Acids and Bases • Chemical Formulas • Reactions, and Relationships • Atomic Structure • Energy and Matter • Elements and Periodic Table	**Government** • Foundations of Govt • Articles of Confederation • The Constitution and Bill of Rights • Three Branches of Govt. • State and Local Govt. • Key Supreme Court Cases • Civil and Criminal Law • Domestic and Foreign Policy	**English 10** English 9 Plus • Debates • Oral Presentations • Socratic Seminars • Poetic Devices • Figurative Language • Word Choice	**Geometry** • Theorems • Triangles and Circles • Geometric Relationships • Formal Mathematical Arguments
11th Grade	**Earth and Space** • Ecological Systems • Cycles of Life and Biosphere • Gravitational Forces • Meteorology • Climatology • Oceanography • Mineralogy • Astronomy • Volcanism	**World History** • Foundations of Civilization • The Renaissance and Reformation • Scientific Revolution • Age of Exploration • Imperialism/Colonization • World Wars I and II • Russian Revolution • The Cold War • Terrorism and the Modern World	**English 11** English 10 Plus • Proper Citations • Foundational US Documents • Informative Writing • Short Stories	**Calculus** • Function Properties • Trigonometry • Conic Sections • Limits, Derivatives • Integration
12th Grade	**Physics** • Atomic Physics and Structure • Light • Wave Mechanics • Alternating/Direct Currents • Electromagnetic Fields • Energy • Heat • Motion • Sound	**Philosophy** • Famous Philosophers • Utilitarianism • Metaphysics • Existentialism • Rationalism • Empiricism • Epistemology • Political Philosophy • Ethics • Logic • Eastern Religions	**English 12** English 11 Plus • Resume Building • Interview Basics • Publication Editing • Writing to Appropriate Audiences	**Statistics** • Probability • Data Collection and Analysis • Technical Writing

Source: Thomas W. McNicholas III, Teacher, South Hagerstown High School, Washington County Public Schools, Maryland.

Art	Music	P.E.	Other	
Art 1 and 2 • Art History • Drawing/Shading • Lines/Shapes • Art Evaluation	**Piano LAB** • Basic Keyboard Fundamentals • How to Read Music • Melodic Lines • Piano Melodies	**PE 1 and 2** • Field Hockey • Volleyball • Basketball • Flag Football • Archery • Soccer	**Health** • Safe Sexual Behavior • Nutrition • Alcohol, and Drugs	**9th Grade**
Photography • Camera Operation • Composition • Lighting • Historical Examples	**Chorus** • Diction • Breath Support • Tone Quality	**Weight Conditioning** • Lifting • Stretching • Flexibility • Progress Monitoring • Free Weights and Weight Machines	**Financial Literacy** • Budgets • Credit and Debit Cards • Investments • Checking and Savings Accounts • Record Keeping	**10th Grade**
Digital Photography • Pixel-Based Design • Pixel-Based Printing • Digital Darkroom Techniques	**Beginning Band** • Musical Form • Terms and Symbols • Instrument Care/Maintenance • Practice Habits	**Personal Life Fitness** • Self-Maintenance Skills • Yoga and Pilates • Badminton • Dancing, Walking	**World Languages** • French • Spanish • Latin • Speaking • Reading • Writing • Culture • Customs • Holidays	**11th Grade**
Art History • Non-European Traditions and Renaissance Period • Folk Art • Architecture	**Orchestra** • Music Theory • Practice Habits • Bow Usage • Articulation • Tone Quality	**Aerobics** • Aerobics and Step Aerobics • Movements to Music Flexibility • Muscle Tone • Cardiovascular Efficiency	**Yearbook** • Artistic Design • Photography • Graphics • Marketing • Entrepreneurship	**12th Grade**

Of course, you can make a questionnaire asking these same questions—what, how many, and when—and then tabulate the responses, but not only are you creating more work, you're also missing a key opportunity. Talking to the educators gives you the opportunity to listen, plan, and collaborate.

The curriculum chart should be one page (8½ by 11) divided by subject and grade level. Delete vague topics, such as "the writing process" or "solving word problems." These terms don't help you select materials. Instead, choose concrete subjects, such as explorers, animals, plants, the Civil War, and American poets. For each subject and grade level, select five to eight topics. In language arts, state the kinds of literature taught—biography, poetry, mystery. Make your chart heavier in social studies and science. If you include art, music, physical education, and the school library, then cite specific artists, sports, musical composers, and literary genres.

To get an idea of how to begin, study the elementary and secondary curriculum charts (figures 2.4 and 2.5) created by two of my graduate candidates. Although these charts span two pages for readability in this book, single page formatting of charts is a best practice for your ease of reference and your community.

Step 4: Identify Your Selection Criteria

The School Library Alignment IV.B.3. states that you should establish your selection criteria. Clarifying your selection criteria helps you to know exactly what you need to purchase. Sharing the criteria may help the learners to know what to expect in the collection. Post the selection criteria in the school library and on the school library website. But don't start from scratch.

A District Selection Criteria Policy

This is an example of an approved school board policy used in a Maryland district.

The following criteria should be considered in the selection of school library materials:

- Curriculum needs of the individual school, staff, and students based on state and national standards
- Recommendations from library selection tools; minimum two positive reviews
- Reading interests, abilities, and developmental levels of students
- Global perspective and/or point of view
- Free from bias and stereotype
- Literary and artistic quality
- Currency and reliability of information

- Scholarship and competence of the author, producer, and/or publisher
- Respect for intellectual freedom and diversity
- Readability
- Requests from administrators, educators, parents, and student learners
- Attractiveness and durability

Nonprint/digital resources should:

- Be approved by the School Library Supervisor
- Be user friendly
- Be relevant to the curriculum
- Present information that is accurate and reliably maintained
- Be organized and include search capabilities and navigational tools that enhance information retrieval
- Provide readable text, attractive graphics, and an appealing layout
- Not duplicate resources already available in the district

Stand on the professional shoulders of your district colleagues and those at ALA. Use your district's board-approved policy for selecting school library materials. Because the policy is official, and you're a district employee, you must follow policy. Also use the ALA Selection & Reconsideration Policy Toolkit for Public, School, & Academic Libraries (ALA 2018). In case you don't have time to read it now, here is the essential information.

ALA Selection & Reconsideration Policy Toolkit for Public, School, & Academic Libraries

The ALA Toolkit's general selection criteria recommend that materials:

- Support and enrich the curriculum and/or students' personal interests and learning
- Meet high standards in literary, artistic, and aesthetic quality; technical aspects; and physical format
- Be appropriate for the subject area and for the age, emotional development, ability level, learning styles, and social, emotional, and intellectual development of the students for whom the materials are selected
- Incorporate accurate and authentic factual content from authoritative sources
- Earn favorable reviews in standard reviewing sources and/or favorable recommendations based on preview and examination of materials by professional personnel
- Exhibit a high degree of potential user appeal and interest
- Represent differing viewpoints on controversial issues

- Provide a global perspective and promote diversity by including materials by authors and illustrators of all cultures
- Include a variety of resources in physical and virtual formats including print and nonprint such as electronic and multimedia (including subscription databases and other online products, e-books, educational games, and other forms of emerging technologies)
- Demonstrate physical format, appearance, and durability suitable to their intended use
- Balance cost with need

The ALA toolkit identifies special considerations for electronic resources:

- Ease of use of the product
- Availability of the information to multiple simultaneous users
- Equipment needed to provide access to the information
- Technical support and training
- Availability of the physical space needed to house and store the information or equipment
- Available in full text

Although you could write criteria for every single type of material you might have, ranging from art prints to videocassettes, that is too much work for too little payback. Focus on books and databases. When purchasing e-books, know what devices they work on and how many users can check out an e-book at the same time.

Here are four basic questions you can use for nearly any purchase:

- Is the item new, and has it received favorable reviews?
- Is the item appropriate for your users?
- Does the item have a pleasing design?
- Is it cost-effective?

Our *National School Library Standards* encourage you to involve your community in the selection process. Although admirable, this approach is time-consuming; you and other educators are already overworked. Kerby opinion alert—instead of organizing a committee and having all the participants read selection resources and debate the pros and cons of specific titles, figure out another way to involve community members that takes less time.

MY PERSONAL SELECTION CRITERIA

» Includes an engaging cover
» Has reader-friendly features (text features, organization of information)
» Targets appropriate ages
» Reflects diversity
» Remains free of bias and prejudice
» Addresses a topic or viewpoint not already included in the school library
  or replaces a dated item
» Meets curriculum needs
» Is award-winning or highly recommended by reputable review sources
» Was created by a well-respected author, illustrator, or publisher

—Jen Yohe, Teacher, Piney Ridge Elementary School,
Carroll County Public Schools, Maryland

Chapter 2—What Should I Learn Next?

In this chapter, what were the most important ideas that surprised or resonated with you?

_____

_____

_____

_____

Figure 2.1 identifies twelve School Library Domains and Alignments that refer to collection development. Identify three critical tasks you need to accomplish.

_____

_____

_____

_____

Create your school analysis, curriculum chart, and selection criteria. Before sharing them with the entire school community, share with a few colleagues and revise using their feedback. What insights about your learners did you discover from this process?

_____

_____

_____

_____

Chapter 2 worksheet supporting *An Introduction to Collection Development for School Librarians* by Mona Kerby, © 2019 American Library Association.

 For a one-page, printable version of this worksheet, go to **alaeditions.org/webextras.**

What Sources Do I Use to Select New Materials?

At some point, expect a classroom educator to hand you a bibliography she received from a conference and ask you to purchase the items. You glance at the list and see dated materials. Hesitate. For one thing, the books may no longer be available, which means you would be wasting your time in preparing the order. Besides, do you really want to spend your small budget on aging materials when you already have plenty of old stuff on the shelves?

Before you make a personal purchase such as a car, a refrigerator, or even a tube of toothpaste, you probably read reviews to make your decision. But the authenticity of those reviews is sometimes questionable because you don't know the reviewers or the criteria they use. When purchasing school library materials, don't waste your limited school funds. Use highly respected, professional selection sources.

By doing so, you're demonstrating School Library Alignments II.C.2. by providing high-quality and high-interest literature and IV.A.2. by ensuring that your resources reflect current knowledge. If you're in graduate school, you may have an assignment using professional selection tools to prepare an order, thereby demonstrating ALA/AASL/CAEP Component 4.2.

A professional selection source reviews *recently* published materials. This means the reviews are written either before the materials are published or soon after publication. The professional selection source provides a variety of ways to search, including year of publication, subject, grade level, and format type. The reviewers may be paid staff or volunteers, but all are trained on how to evaluate quality.

Each professional selection source has unique distinguishing characteristics. By using multiple professional selection sources, you're getting differing opinions and information—which is vital to making wise purchases.

Sometimes school librarians grumble because they are required to have two positive reviews before purchasing. Let's put this requirement in perspective. If you have seen and touched the item, and you know the item will work for your learners, then you're the selection professional—your opinion is enough. Period.

But if you haven't seen the item, then the reviews are critical. I've been burned by buying books that had just one positive review. Kerby opinion alert—don't buy books unless you've found at least three positive reviews.

But as soon as I say that, know you'll be lucky to get one review for multimedia items. Find one positive review, then read between the lines to see if the multimedia item meets your learners' needs.

Some school librarians say they don't use professional selection sources because they don't want to spend the money on "themselves." That argument doesn't make a lick of sense. That's penny-wise and pound-foolish. Please—set aside money to purchase the sources.

To order the school library materials, you work with your vendor or jobber. A jobber is a "middleman" company between you and all the publishers. A jobber saves you time because you prepare one order instead of multiple orders to many publishers. Usually your district will tell you which jobber to use. Examples are Baker & Taylor, Follett, Ingram, and Mackin—each saves you precious time. Another reason to use a jobber is the additional services it provides. For a reasonable fee, the jobber will process and catalog the books and attach spine labels, bar codes, and plastic covers.

When selecting the titles from your jobber, always use the ISBNs for library bindings. The cost is the same as the bookstore option, but the library bindings have a few more stitches, which means the books last longer. Try not to buy a book from a bookstore because the binding may not last longer than four or five reads. In your jobber options, you will see the trade ISBN and the ISBN for library bindings. Choose the latter.

Remember jobbers are out to make money. They are only going to warehouse materials they think they can sell. This means you may order some titles that aren't in the warehouse. Many school librarians are instructed by their supervisors to over-order from the jobber—more than twice the number of titles they have the money for. On their orders, they include a statement such as, "Fill to, but do not exceed, _____ amount." In recent years, the need to over-order has become less of a problem, but do check with your school library supervisor.

If you are ordering books that are going to be read over many years—perhaps classroom sets—then consider purchasing them from companies such as Perma-Bound or Bound to Stay Bound Books. These books are nearly indestructible; their covers can survive being attacked by teething puppies and being run over by trucks. Know that these companies' books are pricey and aren't always pretty.

But back to your jobber. The jobber's software allows you to adjust the settings so you're selecting only items that have multiple reviews. That's a terrific feature, with a big *but*. If you don't know the selection sources, then you don't know which ones to trust. Some professional selection sources include positive *and* negative reviews, so please scan the reviews before selecting the item.

What sources should you use to select new materials? When I was in graduate school, I had to memorize one hundred sources. That's not happening here. As you know, my purpose is to save you time. I recommend three—*Booklist, Horn Book Guide,* and *School Library Journal.* They'll provide an excellent balance of unique perspectives. Much of the following wording comes directly from the sources. Please learn the distinguishing characteristics of each source.

Booklist

Published in Chicago by the American Library Association for more than one hundred years, *Booklist* helps school librarians and librarians in public libraries by providing reviews of new materials (primarily books, audiobooks, video, and reference sources), readers' advisory, collection development, and professional development. *Booklist* comprises two print magazines, an extensive website and database, e-newsletters, webinars, and other resources that support librarians in collection development.

Key Features of *Booklist*

- Available as a print magazine published twice monthly and an extensive searchable online database.
- Reviews new books and audiobooks, ranging in age from preK to adult; also reviews reference materials; databases are reviewed semiannually; approximately two thousand reviews yearly for school-age readers.
- Reviews constitute a recommendation for purchase; about 175–225 words per review.
- Other features include *Book Links,* articles, webinars, and recommended bibliographies.
- *Booklist* magazine is published twenty-two times a year and reviews some eight thousand new materials yearly. The reviews span all ages, from the very young to adult. In addition to the reviews, there are a variety of lists, including best books of the year, top ten lists for multiple genres, adult titles recommended for teens, and the year's best reference materials.
- *Book Links* is published four times a year and provides comprehensive information on using books in the classroom, including thematic bibliographies with related discussion questions and activities, author and illustrator interviews, and articles by educators on practical ways to turn children on to reading.
- Booklist Professional Development: *Booklist* offers three to five webinars monthly on such topics as curriculum design, how to increase reading rates, seasonal features, and publishing previews sponsored by various publishing houses and

imprints. Anyone can sign up for a *Booklist* webinar, regardless of whether they subscribe to the publication. *Booklist* has newsletters, e-mail blasts, and a blog for librarians and book lovers called *The Booklist Reader.*

• Booklist Online: In addition to archived articles, Booklist Online includes a growing archive of more than 180,000 reviews, searchable by year published, age or grade level, topic, and broad areas such as Adult Nonfiction, Adult Fiction, Youth Nonfiction, Youth Fiction, Adult Audio and Video, and Youth Audio and Video.

How Reviews Are Written

Booklist reviews are considered the "haiku" of book reviewing. *Booklist* follows a "recommended-only" policy, which means that every title reviewed would make a quality addition to library collections. This positive review means the material is well written, well researched, and artistically successful. Sometimes *Booklist* recommends titles anticipated to have reader interest that don't meet this high standard, but the review explains the rationale for inclusion.

Book reviews average 175–225 words in length. Reviewers provide a recommended age or grade level, put the book in context, suggest the plot without giving much away, identify the appropriate audience, write in a lively and engaging fashion, and offer a judgment that identifies the book's strengths and weaknesses. Starred reviews indicate titles exceptional in genre or format.

Reference materials are found in the adult nonfiction section of *Booklist*. Electronic reference sources, such as databases, are examined semiannually in the "E-Reference Update." Reviewers note such things as indexes, illustrations, and other text features, as well as judging whether the work fulfills the stated purpose and meets the audience's needs.

Reviewers of audiobooks focus on the narration and why audio for the title is an excellent format choice.

Cost

The cost for an individual annual subscription is $167.50. Bulk discounts are available for school districts. There are occasional specials, such as reduced rates for ALA conference attendees.

Horn Book Guide

Owned by Media Source and published in Boston, the *Horn Book Guide* is not to be confused with its sister publication, *Horn Book Magazine.* Published twice a year, in the fall and the spring, the *Guide* reviews more than two thousand titles, virtually every children's and young adult hardcover trade book published in the United States in a six-month period. The online database includes some 115,000 book reviews that go back to 1989.

Key Features of the *Horn Book Guide*

- Print guide of some two thousand reviews is published every fall and spring; it also has a searchable database.
- Reviews books for ages ranging from preK to teen.
- Reviews are short, critical, and to the point, averaging fifty words in length; ranks books on a 1–6 scale.
- Cost-effective.

How Reviews Are Written

Reviews save you time because they are succinct, yet comprehensive. Each book is rated using the following criteria:

1 = Outstanding, noteworthy in style, content, and/or illustration
2 = Superior, well above average
3 = Recommended, satisfactory in style, content, and/or illustration
4 = Recommended, with minor flaws
5 = Marginal, seriously flawed, but with some redeeming quality
6 = Unacceptable in style, content, and/or illustration

In a typical issue of the *Guide,* you can expect the following distribution of ratings:

1 percent of the books receiving the highest level of 1
8 percent receiving a 2
40 percent receiving a 3
32 percent receiving a 4
17 percent receiving a 5
2 percent receiving a 6

The following grade levels are used for fiction in the *Guide:*

Preschool = birth to age 4
Picture Books = grades K–3
Easy Readers = grades K–3
Younger Fiction = grades 1–3

Intermediate Fiction = grades 4–6
Older Fiction = young adult (grades 7 and up)

The page layout is easy to read, with a triangle symbol marking the titles that receive superior ratings of 1 or 2. The indexes are terrific—search by subject, series, title, author, illustrator, and new editions.

Cost

The cost for an individual annual subscription is less than $50.00. Look for bulk subscription rates and frequent sales, which make this affordable price even lower.

READING SELECTION SOURCES DIGITALLY

I read *School Library Journal* on my iPad via our district's e-magazine platform. The articles keep me up to date with the library world. I like how the reviews in the back are organized by grade and type. I read the Verdicts first and decide whether to read the complete reviews. I keep an ongoing list so purchasing materials doesn't seem like such a large task.

—Ariel Kifer, School Librarian, Williamsport High School,
Washington County Schools, Maryland

School Library Journal

With home offices in New York City and owned by Media Sources, *School Library Journal* (*SLJ*) was established in 1954. Now, with more than 100,000 subscribers, *SLJ* is the premier publication for school librarians and public librarians who work with children and teens. The monthly magazine includes articles covering literacy, best practices, technology, multimedia, education policy, and other issues of interest to the school library and greater educator community. The magazine releases a variety of "best of the year" lists on books and multimedia. *Series Made Simple* is a semiannual supplement that features reviews of series nonfiction books.

Key Features of *School Library Journal*

- Available as a monthly print magazine and an extensive searchable online database.
- Focus is on school and public librarians who work with children and teens; has helpful articles covering literacy, best practices, technology, multimedia, and education policy; provides multiple recommended bibliographies and webinars; semiannual supplement features reviews of series nonfiction books.
- Reviews are 250 words long, written by volunteers, and may be positive or negative.
- Reviews fiction, nonfiction, graphic novels, multimedia, digital, and professional reading for librarians; about six thousand reviews yearly.

Each issue includes reviews of materials for ages birth to three years, three to five years, elementary, tweens, and teens. Both fiction and nonfiction titles are reviewed, as are graphic novels, multimedia, and digital resources. Also included are reviews of professional reading for librarians and reference books. Each year, *SLJ* publishes some six thousand reviews of the newest materials, which are accessed via the magazine or online database.

How Reviews Are Written

Reviews are written by hundreds of volunteers from all over the country who are practicing librarians, booksellers, or others with expertise in children and literature. (You may want to request to be a reviewer.) Reviewers' names and locations appear at the end of each review.

Reviews can be positive or negative and are not longer than 250 words. A review begins with the recommended grade level, as determined by the reviewer, who does not automatically use the publishers' recommendations. Half the review summarizes or describes the book; the rest is evaluative and critical in nature. The critical evaluation focuses on the overall merits of (or concerns about) the text, the artwork, the design, character development, plot, pacing, and the like and on how those qualities ultimately combine for the intended audience. Each review ends with a Verdict—the statement answers the questions, "Should librarians buy this book? Why or why not? If so, for whom?" In each issue, the *SLJ* Book Review Stars appear on the last page—fifteen to twenty titles. These "Stars" are selected by adapting the Children's Notable Lists guidelines of the Association for Library Service to Children: literary quality; originality of text and illustration; clarity and style of language; excellence of illustration; excellence of design and format; subject matter of interest and value to children; and appeal to intended audience.

Cost

The cost for an individual annual subscription is less than $159 for access to print and digital with rates slightly lower when choosing one format instead of both.

Kirkus

Kirkus is another source to know. I don't recommend subscribing, unless your entire district can get a good price on its database. Instead, adjust your jobber settings so the software pulls up Kirkus reviews. Founded in 1933, Kirkus has been an authoritative voice for eighty years. Published twice monthly, Kirkus also has a searchable database. Kirkus averages seven thousand book reviews yearly for ages preK to adult. Kirkus gives industry professionals a sneak peek at the most notable books being published weeks before they're released. Reviews are trusted, unbiased, and critical. They may be positive or negative.

Voice of Youth Advocates (VOYA)

If you are a middle or high school librarian, you will much enjoy reading the *Voice of Youth Advocates (VOYA)* magazine. Located in Bowie, Maryland, owned by E L Kurdyla Publishing, and founded in 1978, *VOYA* is dedicated to the needs of young adult librarians, the advocacy of teens and their rights to intellectual freedom and equal access to information, and the promotion of young adult literature and reading. *VOYA* is published six times a year, and each issue includes articles, regular columns, and reviews. Each issue has approximately 350 reviews, totaling more than 2,200 yearly. Volunteers write the reviews. (You may want to volunteer.) Materials being reviewed are given a recommended level of middle school, junior high, high school, and adult books recommended for young adults. Each book is rated using *VOYA*'s unique and valued Q and P rating system whereby Quality and Popularity are ranked on a scale of 1 (lowest) to 5 (highest); the 5Q rating means "hard to imagine being better written," and the 1Q rating means "hard to understand how it got published." The Popularity scale ranges from 5P, meaning "every young adult who reads it was dying to read it *yesterday!*," to 1P, meaning "no YA will read unless forced to for assignments."

Chapter 3—What Sources Do I Use to Select New Materials?

In this chapter, what were the most important ideas that surprised or resonated with you?

_____

_____

_____

_____

State the distinguishing characteristics of the professional selection sources you'll be using. What are their strengths and weaknesses? How much will they cost? What's your plan for paying for them?

_____

_____

_____

_____

Explore the automated settings for your jobber. Jot down the key things you want to remember.

_____

_____

_____

_____

Chapter 3 worksheet supporting _An Introduction to Collection Development for School Librarians_ by Mona Kerby, © 2019 American Library Association.

 For a one-page, printable version of this worksheet, go to **alaeditions.org/webextras.**

What Sources Do I Use to Fill In Collection Gaps?

Things change—learners, curriculum, instructional strategies. Even on the slim chance you inherited a great collection, expect to find areas where you need additional titles or formats.

For example, if you discover you don't have enough materials for all the third-grade learners to complete their independent research projects on planets, then use the jobber's software and tinker with the settings for grade level, number of positive reviews, and items published recently. For digital materials, use the extensive and highly searchable databases of *Booklist* and *School Library Journal.*

Don't buy materials if they're older than three years. Your collection needs to be "of sufficient breadth and currency" (AASL 2018, School Library IV.D.2.). Although there may be exceptions for currency, especially if you need to replace favorite fiction authors, do hesitate before purchasing older materials. Trust me—you'll have plenty of outdated materials. Besides, kids don't check out old materials. Just look at the age of the books on the shelving cart next to the circulation desk, and I've proved my point.

For whatever strange reason, publishers will often release books on the same topic during the same year. Then the topic will disappear for a few years. If you need that topic, and all the titles receive outstanding reviews, buy them.

Still, despite your good efforts in selecting materials, you will miss some great books. Here's my suggestion. If your district can afford it, subscribe to the H. W. Wilson Core Collections database. Also, use yearly recommended lists of materials selected by professional organizations. The good news is that most lists are free.

H. W. Wilson Core Collections

With editorial content provided by both EBSCO and Grey House Publishing, and available in print and databases, the Core Collections are terrific. They are updated weekly. The expert advisory selection committee uses four levels of criteria: of Most Highly Recommended, Core Collection, Supplementary Materials, and Archival Materials. Kerby opinion alert—if the item is *not* Most Highly Recommended, don't buy the item. You can easily search the databases by publication date, age level, and Most Highly Recommended titles. Every item has a book cover image as well as the full reviews from all major professional selection sources. But the databases are expensive. That's why I recommend purchasing database access at the district level for all the school librarians to use.

Children's Core Collection—With forty-nine thousand titles, the database provides recommendations in fiction, nonfiction works, story collections, and picture books for preschool through sixth-grade learners. In addition, the database includes professional literature for children's librarians.

Middle & Junior High School Core Collection—More than thirty thousand recommended fiction and nonfiction books for learners in grades 5 through 9.

Senior High Core Collection—More than thirty thousand recommended fiction and nonfiction books for learners in grades 9 through 12.

Graphic Novels Core Collection—Highlights 3,500 recommended fiction and nonfiction graphic novels in a wide variety of genres, including adventure, biography, fantasy, superhero, horror, mystery, romance, and science fiction. To best facilitate collection development for age-appropriate content, the *Graphic Novels Core Collection* is searchable by the grade levels PreK–grade 5, grades 6–8, grades 9–12, and Adults.

ALA LISTS I USE

When preparing the order, I begin with the Newbery and Caldecott lists. Next, I review the Pura Belpré and Coretta Scott King awards for diversity. The awards guarantee quality and ensure that the books will circulate.

—Lynn Wilcox, School Librarian, Williamsport Elementary School, Washington County Public Schools, Maryland

American Library Association Recommended Yearly Lists

Trust our professional association; you'll find plenty of recommended titles to purchase. Items are selected by committees of volunteer members who are experienced librarians. These lists are published yearly, which means all the titles have been published in the preceding year. Just remember you're not getting the newest materials; use the lists to catch the good titles you missed. Because these items appear on the ALA lists and have been selected by experienced librarians using selection criteria, there is no need to find additional reviews. Still, don't automatically purchase a title just because the item appears on an official-looking list. You're the expert on your learners; make a judgment.

There are several ways to search. You can go to the ALA website and search the terms "ALA Book, Print & Media Awards" and "ALA Recommended Print/Media List." You also can go to the home pages of AASL, the Association for Library Service to Children (ALSC), and the Young Adult Library Services Association (YALSA). Here is what you can expect to find on the ALSC and YALSA web pages.

ALSC Book and Media Awards

- Batchelder
- Belpré
- Caldecott
- Geisel
- Newbery
- Odyssey
- Sibert
- Wilder
- Awards by other organizations (Such a helpful resource!)
- Children's Notable Lists
  - Notable Children's Books
  - Notable Children's Recordings
  - Notable Children's Digital Media

YALSA Book and Media Awards for Libraries

Book Awards
- Alex Awards
- Edwards Award
- Morris Award
- Nonfiction Award
- Odyssey Award
- Printz Award

Selected Book and Media Lists

- Amazing Audiobooks for Young Adults
- Best Fiction for Young Adults
- Great Graphic Novels for Teens
- Outstanding Books for the College Bound
- Quick Picks for Reluctant Young Adult Readers
- Teens' Top Ten

YALSA also provides a Teen Book Finder App & Database, which is a one-stop shop for finding selected lists and award winners. Users can search this free resource by award, list name, year, author, genre, and more, as well as print customizable lists.

PRINTZ AND ALEX AWARDS

YALSA sponsors some fantastic awards, and I always look at its list of award winners each year to purchase books for our collection. The Printz and Alex Awards winners and Honor books are always at the top of the list.

—Danielle DuPuis, School Librarian, Hammond High School,
Howard County Public Schools, Maryland

Top Ten Recommendations for Diverse Needs

The following ten recommendations help you meet the needs of many learners, again verifying that you are meeting "the diverse developmental, cultural, social, and linguistic needs" and interests of all learners in your community (AASL 2018, School Library II.B.1.). "The school library facilitates opportunities to experience diverse ideas by constructing a learning environment that fosters the sharing of a wide range of viewpoints and ideas" (AASL 2018, School Library II.C.3.). Supporting balanced perspectives by providing a comprehensive collection is essential to building empathy and equity for learners in a global learning community (AASL 2018, School Library II.A.3., II.D.1.).

Your collection should include and be supported by reliable hardware and software. You must enhance the information, media, visual, and technical literacies of all members of the school community by providing opportunities for creating knowledge through technology (AASL 2018, School Library III.A.2., V.A.2.).

AASL Best Apps for Teaching and Learning—A yearly list of apps of exceptional value for inquiry-based teaching. The lists are announced at ALA's summer conference. There is always a program scheduled during which the committee shares each source. The committee provides bookmarks and presentations for you to use in your own building. Kerby opinion alert—use this list and the one following. Teaching your learners about these yearly resources ensures that everyone stays current with technology.

AASL Best Websites for Teaching and Learning—A yearly list of websites, tools, and resources of exceptional value for inquiry-based teaching and learning. Sites recognized foster the qualities of innovation, creativity, active participation, and collaboration. The free, web-based sites are user friendly and encourage learners to explore and discover.

ALSC Children's Notable Lists for Books, Recordings, and Digital Media—These *three* lists are announced every January. Brief annotations and ordering information are included. The current year's Newbery, Caldecott, Belpré, Sibert, Geisel, and Batchelder Award and Honor books automatically are added to the Notable Children's Books list; however, not all lists that you need are included.

Amelia Bloomer Book List—An annual annotated bibliography of books with significant feminist content, intended for young readers (ages birth through 18).

Coretta Scott King Book Award—Given annually to outstanding African American authors and illustrators of books for children and young adults that demonstrate an appreciation of African American culture and universal human values.

Rainbow Book List—An annual bibliography of quality books with significant and authentic lesbian, gay, bisexual, transgender, and queer or questioning (LGBTQ) content and which are recommended for people from birth through 18 years of age.

Robert F. Sibert Informational Book Medal—Honors the year's most distinguished informational book for children and young adults.

Schneider Family Book Award—A yearly award for an author or illustrator of a book that embodies an artistic expression of the disability experience for child and adolescent audiences.

Stonewall Book Award—A yearly award for books that have exceptional merit relating to the LGBTQ experience.

University Press Books for Public and Secondary School Libraries—This annual tool, published by the Association of University Presses with the support of two ALA divisions—AASL and the Collection Development and Evaluation Section of the Reference and User Services Association (RUSA/CODES)—is for public and secondary school librarians seeking the best nonfiction titles from university press publishers. Book entries include key bibliographic data, a thumbnail description, and an AASL or RUSA/CODES (or both) reviewer rating.

Other Professional Lists and Nonprofit Organizations

Several professional organizations have volunteer book committees that select recommended titles from the current year. Remember, however, to get multiple reviews before purchasing. One favorable review is no guarantee that your learners will check out the item.

Best STEM Books K–12—A joint project of the American Society for Engineering Education, the International Technology and Engineering Educators Association, the National Science Teachers Association, the Society of Elementary Presidential Awardees, and the Children's Book Council, this list of thirty-one books aims to provide recommendations to educators, librarians, parents, and guardians for the best children's books with STEM content.

Children's Choices Reading List—Sponsored by the International Literacy Association and the Children's Book Council, Children's Choices is a reading list with a twist—children themselves evaluate the books and vote for their favorites.

Notable Books for a Global Society—A committee of the International Literacy Association selects twenty-five outstanding trade books for K–12 learners that enhance understanding of people and cultures throughout the world.

Notable Social Studies Trade Books for Young People—Sponsored by the National Council for the Social Studies and the Children's Book Council, this annual bibliography highlights titles for learners in grades K–8 that emphasize human relations, represent a diversity of groups, and are sensitive to a broad range of cultural experiences.

Outstanding Science Trade Books for Students K–12—Sponsored by the National Science Teachers Association and the Children's Book Council, this annual bibliography includes titles in Archaeology, Anthropology, and Paleontology; Biography; Earth and Space Science; Environment and Ecology; Life Science; Physical Science; and Technology and Engineering.

USBBY Outstanding International Books List—The Outstanding International Books (OIB) committee of the United States Board on Books for Young People (USBBY) is charged with selecting international books for young people that are deemed most outstanding of those published during the calendar year. For the purposes of this honor list, the term *international book* is used to describe a book published or distributed in the United States that originated or was first published in a country other than the United States.

Your state reading award selected by students—Most states have yearly awards given by student learners who read from a master list of selected titles (Smith, n.d.). Examples include the Maryland Black-Eyed Susan Book Award sponsored by the Maryland Association of School Librarians, the Pennsylvania Young Reader's Choice Awards Program sponsored by the Pennsylvania School Librarians Association, and the Texas Bluebonnet Award sponsored by the Texas Library Association.

Volunteer committees of librarians select the master lists. Most of the master lists include titles published within the last three years. Although the books will be heavily circulated during the year they are on the master lists, these same titles tend to be ignored in later years, so beware of purchasing too many multiple copies.

Common Sense Media—This nonprofit organization is dedicated to improving the lives of kids and families by providing the trustworthy information, education, and independent voice they need to thrive in the twenty-first century. The website offers independent age-based and educational ratings and reviews for movies, games, apps, TV shows, websites, books, and music.

We Need Diverse Books—This is a nonprofit and grassroots organization of children's book lovers that advocates essential changes in the publishing industry so that all diverse experiences are recognized, including (but not limited to) LGBTQIA, Native, people of color, gender diversity, people with disabilities, and ethnic, cultural, and religious minorities.

Chapter 4—What Sources Do I Use to Fill In Collection Gaps?

In this chapter, what were the most important ideas that surprised or resonated with you?

_____

_____

_____

_____

Explain how your learners' academic and personal needs will influence the professional selection sources you plan to use.

_____

_____

_____

_____

Identify the sources you'll be using and state their advantages and disadvantages. Are there other sources not mentioned that you plan to use? If so, explain your reasons.

_____

_____

_____

_____

Chapter 4 worksheet supporting *An Introduction to Collection Development for School Librarians* by Mona Kerby, © 2019 American Library Association.

 For a one-page, printable version of this worksheet, go to **alaeditions.org/webextras.**

How Do I Weed the Collection?

Librarians tend to be either pack rats or cleaners. I'm a cleaner. But still, I can tell you from personal experience, weeding is tough, especially if you were the one who bought the materials, shared them, and shelved them. Perhaps the reason we use the word *weed* is to remind us that weeding is necessary for new growth.

I know some school librarian pack rats who won't weed because their budgets are small or nonexistent. Although this reason may sound rational, it's not. Other common excuses for not weeding include:

- I don't have time to weed.
- Books are sacred objects.
- Someone may need this in the future.
- I can't decide when fiction is outdated.
- I hate to admit that I made a mistake.
- This is a good book. I remember when I bought it—ten years ago.

When shelves are crammed full of old and tattered books, learners won't touch them. Instead, young learners circle the check-in cart, grabbing the newest titles. The kids look like buzzards hunting for roadkill. Old books are treasures, to be sure. But golden oldies belong in your personal collection and in historical collections in museums, archives, and university libraries—not on school library shelves. Young learners believe that if something is in print, then the words are true. Young learners don't yet have the skills to discriminate between correct and inaccurate information. More than ever before, school librarians must teach learners how to tell truth from lies. Having outdated, inaccurate, culturally insensitive materials is just plain wrong.

GOLDEN OLDIES

What golden oldies need to be weeded from your collection? Here are a few titles my graduate candidates recently found on school library shelves:
» *Biological Science: An Ecological Approach,* 1973
» *Photosynthesis,* 1968
» *Square and Folk Dancing: A Complete Guide for Students,* 1984
» *The World of Physics,* 1972

If anything, your reasons to weed and its benefits should far outweigh any apprehensions. You will create space. Crammed shelves are tough on book bindings. Aim to have shelves one-half to three-quarters full. You will save time for learners and yourself because you'll find materials easier. You will enhance your reputation. If the school library is neat, organized, and attractive, learners understand that you value reading, learning, and learners—actions speak louder than words. You'll find that circulation increases after you remove unattractive books. What's more, you learn the collection, identifying its strengths and weaknesses (Larson & Texas State Library and Archives Commission 2012, 16–17).

Policy

How do you know what to weed? As noted in chapter 1, review your district board–approved weeding policy. For example, the policy might say, "As school library materials become dated, damaged, or lost, the school librarian along with other appropriate staff members will determine if (a) the item is still available and can be replaced; (b) a newer item might be a better choice; (c) the item is still needed by the community; and (d) the Internet or interlibrary loan can provide a superior selection."

See how this brief statement puts things in perspective? You're not throwing stuff away willy-nilly; you're improving the collection. Because it's a board policy, you are doing your job. Your principal will support you, instead of doubting your sanity.

Your weeding efforts are also supported by the *National School Library Standards,* when adopting and employing a dynamic collection policy and plan "that includes selection and retention criteria for all materials within the collection" (AASL 2018, School Library IV.B.3.), ensuring that "resources reflect current and in-depth knowledge" (AASL 2018, School Library IV.A.2.). Your use of evaluation criteria equally meets the ALA/AASL/CAEP Components 4.2 Information Resources and 5.3 Advocacy, when you use policies and procedures to manage the school library.

Who Weeds?

You do. Do not ask parents, student learners, or classroom educators to help. Their belief that books are sacred will hamper the task. Besides, this is your responsibility. You know everyone in the building; you know the curriculum; and, because you read selection sources, you know what kinds of new materials are available. You're thinking of all these factors as you make decisions. If possible, team with another school librarian from a nearby school. Not only can your friend tease you in case you stubbornly want to hang on to outdated titles, but when you return the favor, you get to examine her collection.

If you weed in one long session, don't leave the boxes in sight; weeding can upset people. You'll attract less notice by scheduling smaller sessions and by weeding after school. Whatever you do, don't shut the school library or cancel classes. That is denying access to information—making you a very unpopular person.

CURDLED MILK

The milk in the refrigerator is outdated, curdled, and lumpy. Would you:

» Keep it because you don't know when you can get to the store?
» Give it to a neighbor to keep in her house?
» Keep it because otherwise the refrigerator would be empty?

—Gail Dickinson, PhD, Old Dominion University, Norfolk, Virginia

---

Basic Weeding Guidelines

Using your automated circulation system, print out a variety of reports. You want to see the copyright years of all the materials. You also want to know the circulation records of all materials. You'll be examining the oldest items and the ones that have not circulated in a certain amount of time, usually within the last three years.

Spend time sitting in front of the shelves and physically examining the books. Ask yourself questions. How old is the book? Are the information and pictures current? Does it need repair, perhaps a new plastic cover? Is it a popular book that needs to be replaced? Is this a good book we've ignored, and I need to display it? Ahead of time, prepare some paper slips with the headings Mend, Discard, Replace, or Display, and insert the appropriate slip in each book.

When you're deciding what to discard, consider deleting items that fall in the following categories (Larson & Texas State Library and Archives Commission 2012, 19–20):

- Are **outdated** or **incorrect**, especially about computers, community helpers, law, science, space, health, technology, geography, travel, and transportation
- Aren't found as recommended in a **retrospective selection source**
- Don't match the **curriculum** or **learner interests**
- Haven't **circulated** in three to five years
- Are unneeded **duplicates** or can be obtained quickly in another format
- Are **ugly**—dirty, missing pages, poorly bound, have unattractive covers, or have a poor-quality page layout

CREW and MUSTIE Explained

One of our most important resources is freely available on the Internet as a downloadable PDF. Published by the Texas State Library and Archives Commission, *CREW: A Weeding Manual for Modern Libraries* was revised and updated in 2012. CREW stands for **C**ontinuous **R**eview, **E**valuation, and **W**eeding, and the CREW guidelines are based on years of professional experience and best practices. The guidelines include recommendations for every section of the library, including e-books and multimedia. CREW uses a formula based on three factors—the age of the item, when it last circulated, and the MUSTIE criteria.

A MUSTIE formula follows this format: X/X/MUSTIE. The first figure is the item's age. The second figure refers to how many years it has been since the item was last checked out. The third component stands for the six negative MUSTIE factors (Larson & Texas State Library and Archives Commission 2012, 52–59):

- *Misleading* (or factually inaccurate). Weed outdated editions and books that are no longer accurate. Pay special attention to areas in which information has changed recently or in which the information changes rapidly, such as medicine and travel.
- *Ugly* (worn and beyond mending).
- *Superseded* (by a new edition or a better book on the subject). This is especially true for reference materials and test guides.
- *Trivial* (of no discernible literary or scientific merit; usually of ephemeral interest at some time in the past). Weed older titles that reflect outdated popular culture.
- *Irrelevant* to the needs and interests of your learners.
- *Elsewhere* tells us that the material or information may be obtained expeditiously elsewhere via electronic format or interlibrary loan.

So, a formula of 5/3/MUSTIE means that if the item is five years old, has not been checked out in three years, and meets one or more of the MUSTIE factors, then that item should be considered for discarding.

Study the chart I created based on the MUSTIE formulas (figure 5.1). The CREW instructions remind you to use professional judgment and common sense when weeding. This means you can adapt the formulas to your needs.

How Many, How Often, and When?

Instead of weeding the entire school library every year, focus on different sections. Again, in your school library handbook, you should find what sections to weed and when. Feel free to use the Weeding Schedule in figure 5.2.

If you inherit an aging collection, you may really need to weed the entire school library during the first year, but do try to find an experienced school librarian to help you. I still regret deleting some out-of-print classics that were used—and beloved—by our second-grade educator.

FIND THE WEEDS

Weed the collection? The question in your first year is, can you identify the weeds from the blooms? Put this necessary task off until the spring. By then you'll have a better sense of what is getting used by whom.

—Jeanne Mayo, School Librarian, Liberty High School,
Carroll County Public Schools, Maryland

After you get the school library in good shape, how many items should be deleted each year? At Little School where I had ten thousand books, I deleted some three hundred to four hundred books yearly. I made decisions on about seventy-five to one hundred titles at the circulation desk. The books were damaged in some way—chewed by dogs, left out in the rain, run over by cars.

At the circulation desk, grab the books needing new plastic covers or mending and take care of those weekly. Purchase covers, book attaching tape, and mending tape from a library supply company. This effort really spiffs up a collection.

FIGURE 5.1

CREW Weeding Guidelines for Fiction, Nonfiction, Multimedia, and E-books

Section	Formula	Guidelines
Picture Books	X/2/MUSTIE	Evaluate *carefully* using MUSTIE as a guide. Replace popular titles that are worn. Weed any book that has not circulated in the past 2 years. Picture books are so heavily used that every title should go out at least once in a 2-year period. Weed books that reflect racial and gender bias.
Fiction	X/2/MUSTIE	Evaluate for MUSTIE factors. Consider weeding anything that hasn't circulated in the past 2 years. Weed primarily based on current interest except award books and those on school lists.
YA Fiction	3/2/MUSTIE	Any item that has not circulated within 2 years should be considered "dead" and removed (and anything that hasn't circulated within the past year is suspect and should be evaluated for promotion, relocation, or discard).
Graphic Novels	X/1/MUSTIE	Because of their popularity, consider weeding any title that hasn't circulated in the past year. Weed titles that are falling apart.
004 Computers	3/X/MUSTIE	Books on computers are quickly outdated. Consider paperbacks or databases.
Other 000s	5/X/MUSTIE	Weed outdated encyclopedias, atlases, almanacs, and dictionaries, and direct users to databases. Books of oddities and the unexplained, including books on UFOs, should be weeded based on interest and MUSTIE factors more than on copyright date.
133 Paranormal	10/3/MUSTIE	Keep until worn. Replace lost and stolen titles regularly.
150 Psychology	10/3/MUSTIE	Weed based on popularity and use.
200 Religion	10/3/MUSTIE or 5/3/MUSTIE	Have something up-to-date on every religion in the school community and the six major international religions: Buddhism, Christianity, Hinduism, Islam, Judaism, and Taoism.
320 Political Science	5/3/MUSTIE	Be aware of changes in political rhetoric, and discard books with outdated ideas.
390–394 Holidays	10/3/MUSTIE	Holiday-specific books may only circulate once or twice a year. Discard books that are MUSTIE or that reflect gender, family, ethnic, or racial bias.
398 Folklore	X/3/MUSTIE	Folktales never go out of date, so weed based on the quality of the retelling, especially if ethnic bias is present. Evaluate for MUSTIE and low circulation.
500	5/3/MUSTIE	Evaluate *all* science books older than 5 years, especially physics, astronomy, environmental issues, dinosaurs, and astronomy. Check books on atoms every two years. Botany doesn't change often and may be older. Keep basic books of significant historical or literary value, such as Darwin's *Origin of Species*.
510 Math	10/3/MUSTIE	Math does not change rapidly, so weed primarily based on MUSTIE factors and lack of use.

(cont.)

Section	Formula	Guidelines
520 Space and Astronomy	5/3/MUSTIE	Weed titles that include Pluto as a planet or that don't include information on the space station and Mars expeditions. Stargazing books may be retained longer but should be attractive and mention relevant technology.
560 Dinosaurs	5/2/MUSTIE	The popularity of topics like dinosaurs may mean that even outdated books are checked out. Discard most books that lack color illustrations.
600	X/3/MUSTIE	Evaluate medicine, health, and space exploration items older than 5 years. Books on gardening may be 10 years old, so circulation is the main weeding criterion. Popular subjects, such as pets and crafts, may need replacing because of worn condition.
700	X/3/MUSTIE	Consider keeping art books. Replace old books on hobbies with current interests. In sports, watch for gender and racial bias. Discard books that have outdated statistics.
800	X/3/MUSTIE	Check with classroom teachers for assignments before discarding. Weed noncirculating poetry and jokes. Regularly replace favorites.
930–999	10/3/MUSTIE	Consider demand and accuracy of facts when reviewing histories.
910 Geography	3/2/MUSTIE	Rotate the purchase of books on countries and states so that no title is older than 5 years.
B or 92 Biography	X/3/MUSTIE	Unless the person treated is of permanent interest or importance, such as a U.S. president, discard a biography as soon as demand lessens. Replace biographies of people of ongoing interest with newer titles at least once a decade because interpretation of their lives and public perception of their impact will change over time.
Multimedia	WORST	Includes a wide variety of formats. Check for items that haven't circulated several times in a year. Use the WORST formula: **W**orn out, **O**ut of date, **R**arely used, **S**upplied elsewhere, or **T**rivial and faddish.
E-books	Use formula for specific fiction or nonfiction.	Electronic materials are still rapidly evolving. Consider the following: What formats are available, and which are needed in the community? Is purchase for unlimited use or for a license limited to a specific number of circulations? Are the e-books included in the online catalog, or must learners use a vendor database?

Source: Chart created by Mona Kerby using *CREW: A Weeding Manual for Modern Libraries* (Larson & Texas State Library and Archives Commission 2012, 61–80).

 For a one-page, printable version of these guidelines, go to **alaeditions.org/webextras.**

FIGURE 5.2

Weeding Schedule

Year ending in:		1	2	3	4	5	6	7	8	9	0
Class	**Interval**										
000	5 years					✓					✓
100	5 years					✓					✓
200	5 years					✓					✓
300	3–4 years			✓			✓				✓
400	5 years	✓					✓				
500	2 years		✓		✓		✓		✓		✓
600	2 years		✓		✓		✓		✓		✓
700	5 years		✓					✓			
800	5 years			✓					✓		
900	3–4 years			✓			✓			✓	
92	3 years	✓			✓			✓			
Easy	5 years		✓					✓			
Fiction	5 years		✓					✓			

Where Do Discards Go?

Beginning librarians worry about this. But know the district library supervisor, not you, establishes the procedures for handling discards. In our school district, we either blacked out the school name or ripped out the pages on which our school name was stamped. We also marked through the computer bar code. As fast as you can, box the books and get them out of the school library, sending them to the appropriate location.

After that, the district decides what to do with them. Most school boards don't give you the authority to give away the books or sell them. Except for rare circumstances, do not give discards to learners. You're going to ignore this suggestion; you can't help yourself. So just know this—if you give those old books to learners, those discarded items will keep coming back to the school library—again and again.

Chapter 5—How Do I Weed the Collection?

In this chapter, what were the most important ideas that surprised or resonated with you?

_____

_____

_____

What did you discover after examining the printout reports of your collection by age and circulation?

_____

_____

_____

Will you be able to adhere to the MUSTIE formulas for each section? If you change the formula, identify the section, give the new formula, and explain your reasons for the changes. What will be your MUSTIE formula for Picture Books, Fiction, Fairy Tales, and Graphic Novels?

_____

_____

_____

Explain your plan of action for weeding the collection.

_____

_____

_____

Chapter 5 worksheet supporting _An Introduction to Collection Development for School Librarians_ by Mona Kerby | © 2019 American Library Association.

 For a one-page, printable version of this worksheet, go to **alaeditions.org/webextras.**

How Do I Evaluate the Collection?

Collection development is a gigantic, ever-changing, ongoing intellectual puzzle. You evaluate the collection to determine its currency, its quality, and, in some respects, its quantity. The major pieces include the grade levels in your building; the curriculum; every learner's abilities and interests; the classroom educators' instructional styles; the quality of the items in the collection; the needed and available budget; and what kinds of materials you need so all learners can actively use the collection to demonstrate competency in the six Shared Foundations of our *National School Library Standards.* Whew! That's thousands of things to remember. In this chapter, we'll examine the pieces of collection development, and though we will discuss each piece, there is no order or hierarchy, nor can you tackle any piece in isolation. Every decision affects another piece of the puzzle.

Our Six Shared Foundations

As I've previously mentioned, our *National School Library Standards* lead us to build the collection so that learners *use* it. I've crafted a summary sentence, albeit a long one, that encompasses our charge:

> *All* learners must actively interact with a current and comprehensive school library collection that meets their curriculum and personal interests; the collection provides learners with opportunities to experience diverse opinions, the research process, high-quality literature, and access to information in multiple ways, always demonstrating competency in our six Shared Foundations.

A dynamic collection-development plan ensures breadth and currency in our collections relevant to the curriculum (AASL 2018, School Library IV.A.2., IV.D.2.). Also, the plan supports collaborative engagement in inquiry-based learning opportunities (School Library III.A.2.) and equitable and ethical exploration of diverse ideas and technologies (School Library I.B.1., II.C.3., V.A.2., VI.D.2.).

If you are in graduate school, you will likely have an assignment to meet ALA/AASL/CAEP Standard 4: Organization and Access whereby you evaluate school library resources.

Personal Interests and Needs of the Learners

So far, we've focused on meeting curriculum needs, but we must always entice learners to read for enjoyment. Don't underestimate the power of reading for pleasure. If we don't instill that love, then our efforts are wasted. Although you can certainly ask learners to complete interest surveys, you will know what to buy for them because you are "fostering opportunities for learners to demonstrate personal curiosity" (AASL 2018, School Library V.A.2.). Plus, by reading professional selection journals and attending professional conferences and webinars, you're keeping up with popular trends.

For educators' needs—hesitate before purchasing professional books because the books will rarely circulate. Instead, spend your efforts in teaching other educators how to use the latest instructional technology tools to enable the generation and creation of new knowledge (AASL 2018, School Library I.B.1., V.A.2.).

Automatic Circulation System Reports

Conducting a collection analysis begins with your automatic circulation system. For our purposes, prepare a report (figure 6.1) for fiction and the ten major Dewey sections that tallies the number of items, the circulation, and the average copyright age.

This analysis will be eye-opening and, most likely, distressing. For one thing, the chart shows just how old your collection is. For another thing, you'll discover you don't have an easy way to count the circulation of e-books. And, finally, I'll bet a nickel your MARC records are a mess. Items may be incorrectly cataloged. Deleted items may still be showing up. Your graphic novels may be cataloged in fiction, the 700s, or somewhere else entirely. Cleaning up those MARC records can take months; the task is thankless but important to do. If you don't clean up the mess, the learners can't access what they need.

FIGURE 6.1

Collection Analysis Overview Chart

Category	Number of Items	Percentage of Total Collection	Average Age	Circulation	Section needs work? (Y/N)
Reference					
000					
100					
200					
300					
400					
500					
600					
700					
800					
900					
92/920					
Easy					
Fiction					
E-books					
Databases					
TOTAL					

At this point, you may be wondering about quantity and age of school library materials. Hold these questions; I'll come back to them.

Additional Automated Analysis

Book jobbers will analyze your collection free of charge. I'd suggest getting two reports. For example, Follett identifies your percentages of print versus digital items. Mackin recommends how many items to have in every section and an appropriate age of the materials. Of course, jobbers want to sell books, but these recommendations will help with your decisions.

Collection Mapping

There is absolutely no need to have school library materials for every subject on the curriculum chart. Ask the other educators—quickly when you see them in the hall or at lunch, but please, no surveys because they will ignore them—what subjects they need school library materials on. The upside of these informal conversations is that you may unexpectedly entice another educator to work with you.

Use the curriculum map worksheet (figure 6.2) to analyze the different curriculum topics. You'll be making judgment decisions. To determine the level of needed school library support, talk to the classroom educators. Do you need a minimal level—a very few items to support occasional use; a basic level—books and databases to support frequent learner requests; or an extensive level—many books and databases to support comprehensive learner research and projects?

If your circulation software compares your collection to a recommended selection source, terrific. But likely, you'll need to do this task yourself; the task is time-consuming but illuminating. It's the only method you have of determining the *quality* of your collection.

Say you have one hundred astronomy books. Take a 10 percent random sample—ten titles. Look up the titles in a professional selection source. I'd recommend the Wilson Core Collections databases to see if the titles are listed as Most Highly Recommended. In all my years of teaching collection development and having my graduate candidates see how many titles meet the Core Collections criteria for Most Highly Recommended, I have never had a candidate whose collection had even 25 percent of the titles listed as Most Highly Recommended. What does this mean? Thousands of poor-quality books are sitting on school library shelves. Heartbreaking.

If you don't have access to the Core Collections databases, then my next recommendation would be to check the titles in the *Booklist* database; I recommend *Booklist* because its reviews constitute a recommendation for purchase. *School Library Journal* and some other sources give positive and negative recommendations, which means that if you use those databases, then you will have to read the reviews instead of just finding the titles. If you don't have *Booklist,* then figure out how you can examine the reviews via your circulation software.

How Many Items, and How Old Is Old?

In the very early days of school librarianship, AASL provided quantitative standards for school libraries. Now our focus is on qualitative standards and school librarians' assessment of the unique characteristics of their individual communities and

FIGURE 6.2

Curriculum Map Evaluation Worksheet

Use this evaluation worksheet to map and analyze your collection against the different topics present in your school or district curriculum.

A Column—Select a section to evaluate, not the entire collection. You might choose Fiction, 500s–600s, or 900s. You could be more specific and choose 599 Animals or 917 Geography, or you could select topics from the curriculum chart you created.

B Column—Identify the grade level needed for the topic.

C Column—Decide the level of support needed—minimal, basic, or extensive.

D Column—Insert the number of items in the section.

E Column—Insert the average copyright year for the items in the section.

F Column—Determine the percentage of titles recommended by either H. W. Wilson or *Booklist* by taking a random sample and then looking up the reviews.

G Column—Determine how many items to weed.

H Column—Determine how many items to purchase, depending on available quality or new titles.

A	B	C	D	E	F	G	H
Dewey Number or Curriculum Subject	Grade Level	Level of Support	Number of Items	Average Copyright Year	Percentage of Positively Reviewed Titles	Number of Items to Weed	Number of Titles Recommended for Purchase

 For a one-page, printable version of this worksheet, go to **alaeditions.org/webextras.**

curricula. Your state education department may still state how many items to have per student, but most of these recommendations were written decades ago, prior to the digital age.

Despite all these explanations, beginning school librarians still ask how old a school library collection should be. On average—and I mean average—I'd say your collection should not be older than twelve years (figure 6.3). In the real world, this average age will be tough to meet. Maybe you will need to extend that average age to fifteen years. Although science needs to be accurate and current, the poetry section can be older. You might think that Picture Books or Everybody Books can average about twenty years old because of so many favorite classics. But still, I'd say that's probably too old.

FIGURE 6.3

Kerby's Chart of Considerations: Possible Quantities and Ages by Section

Use this chart when making judgments about how to improve your collection. The suggestions are considerations only.

| Category | Grades K–5 | | Grades 6–8 | | Grades 9–12 | |
	Approximate Percentage of Items*	Average Age of Items (Years)**	Percentage of Items	Average Age of Items (Years)	Percentage of Items	Average Age of Items (Years)
000	.5–1	5	1	6	1	7
100	.5–1	11	1	11	1	10
200	.5	11	.5–1	11	.5–1	9
300	6–10	11	7–10	10	10	7
400	.5	12	.5	11	.5	9
500	12.5	8	6–7.5	7	5–6	7
600	5–7	9	5–7	8	5–7	7
700	5.5–8	9	6–8	8	6–8	9
800	2–2.5	11	2.5	7	6–8	13
900	6.5–8	8	12	9	12	9
92/920 **Biography**	5.5	10	9	12	5–9	10
Easy Fiction	28	11	na	na	na	na
Fiction	22	12	38–40	12	26–30	12

*The "Approximate Percentage of Items" is based on Mackin's recommendations and a small group of Maryland school library collections.

**The "Average Age of Items (Years)" comes directly from Mackin. Realistically, you may not be able to meet these averages, but they should help with your decisions for your school library.

Sources: Mackin's 2017 Collection Analysis Recommendations, author's survey of Maryland school library collections in spring 2018, and a chart appearing in Betty Thomas's 2004 textbook, *Administering the School Library Media Center.*

If you have about ten items per student, then you should be fine. I'd suggest that you have half the collection in fiction and half in nonfiction. If you still have a printed reference section, get rid of it. Instead use databases. I'd recommend that elementary school libraries have ten to fifteen databases and that secondary school libraries have about twelve to twenty-five databases.

TWELVE DATABASES I HAVE FOR MY ELEMENTARY SCHOOL

Purchased by the district:

» General reference (*Britannica*) in English and Spanish
» Primary encyclopedia (PebbleGo)
» Emergent intermediate encyclopedia (FactCite 123 from Lincoln Library)
» E-book database (TumbleBooks)
» Database on countries (CultureGrams)
» Image database (ImageQuest)
» Two databases for newspaper/magazine index (SIRS and Explora from EBSCO)

Purchased by PTA and school library funds:

» Nonfiction e-book database (TrueFlix from Scholastic)
» Three intermediate encyclopedias for science and social studies (Pebble-Go Next: Science, American Indian History and States, and Biographies)

Wish List:

» Online almanac database

—Margaret Gaudino, School Library Media Specialist, Strawberry Knoll Elementary School, Montgomery County Public Schools, Maryland

Depending on your learners and access, I'd suggest that at least 10 percent of the collection be e-books—and I expect this number will increase. Cataloging those e-books and figuring out circulation will continue to be problems over the next decade.

About book circulation—those yearly numbers better be high. I've seen some school library circulation records showing that the average number of books checked out per student learner was two—for the entire year. Two books a year is terrible. Let's think about this. There are thirty-eight weeks in the school year. Elementary school learners visit the school library for weekly class. This means they should be checking out a minimum of two books each visit for an average of seventy-six books yearly per learner. But even that number may need to be higher because younger learners need to check out books more often given that their books are so short.

About collecting circulation rates on databases—the rates are nearly impossible to discover. Whenever you talk to sales representatives, mention our dilemma of needing circulation data. Eventually the database companies are bound to respond.

Your Budget and Improvement Plan

Although you can certainly make progress in improving an aging collection, don't expect to have a collection in good shape within a year. You'll need thousands of dollars, and the school won't be able to afford the cost. Besides, in any given year, you won't find enough recently published materials on the curriculum topics you need. Say you need twenty additional astronomy titles for the third-grade research unit. Just so you know—there will not be twenty brand-new astronomy books published this year, and few of them will be high quality. And why buy older mediocre titles? You've got plenty.

To allow for "a dynamic collection-development plan" (AASL 2018, School Library IV.A.2.), consider a three-year plan; even a seven-year plan is reasonable. Every spring, *School Library Journal* announces the average prices of books in the print journal and then makes this information accessible via SLJ Online. Use these prices so you'll have a good estimation of how much money you will need.

Preparing a Formal Report for Your Principal

This report may be the most important one you ever write. A successful report can benefit every learner in your building for years to come. The report describes your aging collection and requests money for improving the collection. Have someone proofread your writing for clarity and for the argument. If your principal asks what you mean, then you didn't write clearly enough. A sample report is shown in figure 6.4.

Your report must be two pages, maximum. One page is better. Your principal is busy; give her only the essential information. If the report is short and powerful, then the principal can easily share it with the PTA or a Booster Club that may have additional funds. In the report, prove that your collection is old and that you need funds. And—let me say this loud and clear—your math had better be correct. This

FIGURE 6.4

Report to Principal

Dear [*Principal*]:

We've just completed an evaluation of the Science/Mathematics section (the 500s of the Dewey Decimal Classification System) in our school library. Unfortunately, we discovered that the average copyright date is 1998. Scientific information is often outdated within five years, but our students are using books with twenty-year-old facts.

This section is heavily used by our learners at every grade level. In addition, our collection isn't adequate for the new curriculum changes. If we want to support our district's initiative to raise standardized test scores, we must provide accurate and up-to-date information.

Here are some additional shocking figures.

- Only 13 percent of our science books were positively reviewed by a professional selection source.*
- To improve the Science section so that it averages fifteen years old instead of twenty years old, we would need to purchase more than five hundred new books costing $9,000!**

Not only is the cost prohibitive but also there aren't five hundred positively reviewed science books published during a year.

After much thought, we are requesting funding of $1,000 for three years. This amount allows us to purchase approximately fifty books yearly as well as several science databases. This amount is in addition to the funds already budgeted for school library books. As you might imagine, we have many outdated books, and we need to improve the entire collection.

Thank you for taking time to examine this report and for any support you can give us in our attempt to provide quality materials for our young scholars. Please feel free to stop by the school library, examine our collection, and ask us questions.

Sincerely,

[*Insert your name*]

*We compared our science books to the H. W. Wilson *Core Collection,* a professional selection source that provides professional reviews, and were dismayed to see that only 13 percent of the titles met the rating of Most Highly Recommended.

**According to the latest *School Library Journal* report, the average cost of a hardback elementary school library book is $18.69.

(*cont.*)

FIGURE 6.4
Report to Principal *(cont.)*

Ten Golden Oldies Still on Our Shelves

CHART 1

Book Name	Copyright Date
A Golden Guide: Seashores	1955
Vulcan—The Story of a Bald Eagle	1955
The First Book of Snakes	1956
Birds: A Golden Guide	1956
Prisms and Lenses	1959
Junior Science Book of Bacteria	1961
Chemistry by Experiment	1965
Strange Companions in Nature	1966
Botany	1970
Today's Biggest Animals	1977

Sixty-Nine Percent of Our Books Are Ten Years Old or Older   CHART 2

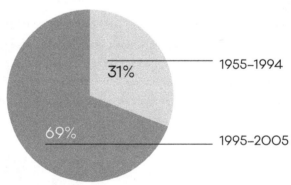

Average Age of Books in Collection 2008-2018

31% — 1955–1994

69% — 1995–2005

Only 13 Percent Match a Professional Selection Source   CHART 3

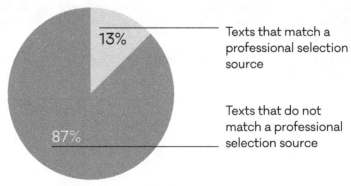

Professional Selection Source Texts

13% — Texts that match a professional selection source

87% — Texts that do not match a professional selection source

is not the time to be making mistakes because the principal will then have a reason to delay funding. Ask for less money than you need. Look reasonable. Think strategically.

Make your charts professional, and include only the most important and shocking information. List a few of the worst titles you found. Highlight how few of your materials are highly recommended in a professional selection source. Some principals don't understand the necessity of your subscribing to professional selection sources, so this is a perfect opportunity to explain why professional selection sources improve the quality of your purchases.

YOUR TURN

Chapter 6—How Do I Evaluate the Collection?

In this chapter, what were the most important ideas that surprised or resonated with you?

_____

_____

_____

_____

_____

Compare your printout reports to Kerby's Chart of Considerations: Possible Quantities and Ages by Section (figure 6.3). What are the strengths and weaknesses of your collection?

_____

_____

_____

_____

_____

What are your steps for improving the collection?

_____

_____

_____

_____

_____

Chapter 6 worksheet supporting _An Introduction to Collection Development for School Librarians_ by Mona Kerby, © 2019 American Library Association.

For a one-page, printable version of this worksheet, go to **alaeditions.org/webextras.**

How Do I Turn a Complaint into a Positive?

I was terrified of having a book challenged. Sometimes I would wake up at night, worrying. I was afraid a parent would be angry with me and my principal would think I was a bad librarian. If you find yourself wide awake one night worrying about this, then get up from bed, drink some water, and read this chapter.

Build Your Foundation before the Complaint Occurs

The first step of preparation is to be an excellent educator. Your lessons will foster "opportunities for learners to demonstrate personal curiosity and creation of knowledge" (AASL 2018, School Library V.A.2.) and "support the diverse developmental, cultural, social, and linguistic needs" represented in your community (AASL 2018, School Library II.B.1.).

Practically speaking, within the first six weeks of school, learn everyone's name. Learn who each learner's brothers and sisters are. Attend PTA meetings and smile. Introduce yourself to parents, expressing your genuine affection for their children. Word gets around. Student learners talk about their educators at the supper table. Parents chat with their neighbors about the school staff. Being a good educator with a loving heart has so many positive repercussions, including making a book challenge a wonderful teaching moment for all.

The second step is to find the section in your district's school library handbook on reconsideration of school library materials. You should see the process, including how the complaint moves up the chain of command. You'll likely see a form, perhaps named "Citizen's Request Form for Reevaluation of School Library Material." Make sure you're reading the section on school library materials, not on text-books. You'll note the complaint begins with the school librarian, not the principal or the superintendent. You will be setting the tone of the conversation, serving as a model of decorum, fairness, and kindness.

HOW COULD ANYONE POSSIBLY COMPLAIN!

Yet if someone does complain, listen and smile and thank her for taking such an active role in education. If she wants to take it farther, explain the procedures. Nine out of ten people will not follow through. (Later, you can call a friend to privately complain about the complainer!)

—Jeanne Mayo, School Librarian, Liberty High School, Carroll County Public Schools, Maryland

The third foundational step is to have a policy allowing all learners the opportunity to come to the school library daily to check out books. When learners don't like the books they checked out, then the learners may return the books immediately—within thirty seconds or sometime that day. This is how your learners learn, by making "mistakes" in their selections. If the learner complains in the classroom or at home about the book, the classroom educator or parent reminds the learner to return the book and select another one. Problem solved.

You are likely to have five to ten books that you "worry" about. They are good books with great reviews, but maybe they've made the news because a community wanted to ban them, or maybe there are a few curse words in the text, or maybe the books deal with an issue that is currently sensitive. Well, let's keep this in perspective. You don't have to advertise that you have the books on the shelves. For heaven's sake, don't delete them from the school library because you're afraid something *might* happen. If you're that worried about the titles, then do some rearranging of the school library shelves and see that the titles are shelved on the bottom shelf somewhere in the middle. When learners only have a few minutes to select books, they go for the top shelves closest to the circulation desk. Still, your worrying will be a waste of time. When parents do come in to "complain," trust me, they will *not* be complaining about one of these books.

Okay. So the parent walks into the school library. Because of your active participation in the community, you already know the parent; you say something nice about her child. Score one point for you. Now the parent starts talking. She may ramble or show a little nervousness. You might be nervous, too, and worried about your voice shaking when you talk. Know how to solve that? Count to five before you open your mouth. Listen. Observe.

You are now in leadership mode. You are modeling our American ideals of freedom of speech. Opinions of authors and opinions of learners should be heard and respected. Your learners have the right to immediately return the book and select another. You are calmly demonstrating that you trust your learners' ability to control the idea, not vice versa—no matter how scary the idea.

MODELING THE SHARED FOUNDATION OF INCLUDE

Model respect for ideas and people; show that the individual controls the idea, not vice versa, no matter how scary the idea.

—Mona Kerby

You may want to suggest that the parent can certainly instruct her child on what to check out, but this is a matter between the parent and child. Offer to make the parent a library card and invite her to check out books. She won't expect that, and you can almost see her modeling your respectful demeanor. Few parents, however, will take you up on the offer.

In most cases, your kindness and willingness to listen result in a win. You will have had a richly rewarding discussion of ideas. The parent will feel validated. The book will stay on the shelf. The matter will end with you.

On rare occasions, a parent will march into the school library, and you can feel her anger. In such times, there's no need to have a lengthy discussion on our American beliefs. Instead, use counseling skills. The school library book has become an easy target, a way to focus frustrations on an object. Something is going on in the parent's life. When I say counseling skills, I don't mean you need to solve a life-problem. I mean stay calm and listen, so the anger will spew out and disperse. After you debrief with your principal, you're likely to learn that the parent is already known for such behavior.

When a person from an organization comes to you to look for "inappropriate" materials, change your tactics. Chances are your district school library supervisor has notified you of the impending visit. In these cases, there is no need to have a discussion. Politely help the person, but the less said, the better.

Afterward, talk to your school library supervisor. She has district-wide experience on these issues; she knows and models our professional code of ethics and beliefs. Of course, you'll talk to your principal, but the principal may not have spent much time thinking about how First Amendment rights apply to student learners, and in the principal's eagerness to solve the problem, she might demand that you get rid of the book. Your school library supervisor will help guide the process.

Know how many challenges I had that moved up the chain of command? Zero. What I'm trying to say is this: please don't censor your collection because you're afraid that a complaint *might* happen.

Professional Statements on Intellectual Freedom

Freedom of speech. First Amendment rights. Intellectual freedom. If you're in graduate school and are not yet a school librarian, you may not have realized your professional role in protecting these rights. Folks may joke about the stereotypical image of librarians who wear glasses, but make no mistake, we are brave souls who champion the American belief that all people have the right to information. Your endorsement of these ideals affects everything in the school library—your lessons, your leadership, and the materials you select.

NATIONAL SCHOOL LIBRARY STANDARDS: COMMON BELIEFS

1. The school library is a unique and essential part of a learning community.
2. Qualified school librarians lead effective school libraries.
3. Learners should be prepared for college, career, and life.
4. Reading is the core of personal and academic competency.
5. Intellectual freedom is every learner's right.
6. Information technologies must be appropriately integrated and equitably available.

Our professional documents are located on the ALA and AASL websites. But because it is easy to get overwhelmed when reading online, I made location maps of what I consider to be the most important titles and how to find them. These documents are so wonderful. Bookmark them and review them frequently. I've chosen several of the documents I consider most essential. For our purposes, I'm only quoting the key ideas. As you read these statements, ponder how you will share this information with your learners.

SCHOOL LIBRARY FIRST PRINCIPLES

- » All learners have the right to use our school library.
- » All learners can select and return books daily.
- » We provide materials that support intellectual growth and individual interests.
- » We provide courteous responses to all requests.
- » We don't charge late fees.
- » We trust our learners to choose their own materials.
- » We don't restrict materials by age, grade, or reading level.
- » We don't require educator or parent approval.
- » We believe parents may choose to restrict the access of their children, but they should so advise their children.
- » We resist all efforts to censor school library materials.
- » We protect our learners' right to privacy and avoid printing class lists of overdue materials to be publicly shared.
- » We believe the freedom to read is essential to our democracy.

—Mona Kerby

The Key ALA Professional Statements and How to Find Them

Many of the following documents can be found on ALA's website (ala.org) under the tab "Advocacy, Legislation & Issues." If a direct link is missing, type the topic into the search box on the home page.

- Banned & Challenged Books
  - Coping with Challenges
    - » Kids and Libraries: What You Should Know
    - » What Is the Library Bill of Rights?

- Equity, Diversity & Inclusion

- Intellectual Freedom
  - Library Bill of Rights: Interpretations of the Library Bill of Rights
    - » Access to Resources and Services in the School Library (2014)
    - » Challenged Resources (2019)
    - » Labeling Systems (2015)
    - » Restricted Access to Library Materials (2014)

- First Amendment and Censorship
- Access to Library Resources and Services
- Filters & Filtering
- Academic Freedom
- Schools and Minors' Rights
  - » Access to Resources and Services in the School Library: An Interpretation of the Library Bill of Rights (2014)
  - » Minors and Internet Activity: An Interpretation of the Library Bill of Rights (2014)
  - » *Defending Frequently Challenged Young Adult Books: A Handbook for Librarians and Educators* (2016) by Pat R. Scales
- Hate Speech and Hate Crime

- Privacy
  - Library Privacy Guidelines
    - » Library Privacy Guidelines for Students in K–12 Schools

Go to the web page "Tools, Publications & Resources"

- Professional Ethics: Code of Ethics

The Key AASL Professional Statements and How to Find Them

Go to the website for the American Association of School Librarians (ala.org/aasl) and select the web page "Advocacy."

- Intellectual Freedom
  - Intellectual Freedom Brochure
  - Material Challenges

- Resources
  - Position Statements
    - » Strategic Leadership Role of School Librarians (2018)

Freedom to Read Statement

The Freedom to Read Statement emphasizes the trust we should place in our learners and how we help them live up to this trust. The essential wording follows.

> The freedom to read is essential to our democracy. It is continuously under attack.
> . . . Most attempts at suppression rest on a denial of the fundamental premise of democracy: that the ordinary citizen, by exercising critical judgment, will accept the good and reject the bad.

The censors, public and private, assume that they should determine what is good and what is bad for their fellow citizens.

> We trust Americans to recognize propaganda and misinformation, and to make their own decisions about what they read and believe.

We do not believe people need the help of censors to assist them in this task.

> Now as always in our history, reading is among our greatest freedoms. . . . The freedom to read is guaranteed by the Constitution. Those with faith in free people will stand firm on these constitutional guarantees of essential rights and will exercise the responsibilities that accompany these rights." (ALA 2004)

ALA Code of Ethics

First written in 1939 before World War II and revised in 2008, the ALA Code of Ethics includes eight principles. Here are four essential responsibilities that school librarians demonstrate.

> [W]e are members of a profession explicitly committed to intellectual freedom and the freedom of access to information. We have a special obligation to ensure the free flow of information and ideas to present and future generations.

> 1. We provide the highest level of service . . . through appropriate and usefully organized resources; equitable service policies; equitable access; and accurate, unbiased, and courteous responses to all requests.
> 2. We uphold the principles of intellectual freedom and resist all efforts to censor library resources.
> 3. We protect each library user's right to privacy and confidentiality with respect to information sought or received and resources consulted, borrowed, acquired or transmitted . . .
> 4. We . . . do not allow our personal beliefs to interfere with fair representation of the aims of our institutions or the provision of access to their information resources. (ALA 2008)

Library Bill of Rights

Also written in 1939 on the eve of world war, the Library Bill of Rights supports our steadfast belief that ideas must not be censored. In our current environment where politicians demean truth, the Library Bill of Rights becomes essential for our learners.

The Bill of Rights includes seven ideas. Here are three of them.

1. Books and other library resources should be provided for the interest, information, and enlightenment of all people of the community the library serves. Materials should not be excluded because of the origin, background, or views of those contributing to their creation.
2. Materials should not be proscribed or removed because of partisan or doctrinal disapproval.
3. Libraries should challenge censorship in the fulfillment of their responsibility to provide information and enlightenment. (ALA 1996)

A HIGH SCHOOL LIBRARIAN'S EXEMPLAR

You have the freedom to:
» Read and enjoy whatever is interesting to you—books, magazines, websites, databases!
» Use our school library to help you learn, discover, escape, create, and experience the world.
» Find characters and opinions that are as diverse as our school and world.

My pledge:
» I will show you how to respect others by respecting you.
» I will read books that are interesting to you, and I'll always keep learning.
» I will use my librarian powers to get the best books and materials for you.
» I will teach you how to find the information you need.
» I will help you, even if I look busy. You are the most important part of my job.

Note: Rights paraphrased from ALA's Freedom to Read Statement and pledge paraphrased from ALSC's Core Competencies.

—Katie Florida, School Librarian, Oakland Mills High School, Howard County Public Schools, Maryland

The Library Bill of Rights for School Libraries

First written in 1986 and last revised in 2014, *Access to Resources and Services in the School Library Program: An Interpretation of the Library Bill of Rights* explains our mission as school librarians. The one-page PDF may be duplicated for your learners. The essential ideas follow.

> The school library plays a unique role in promoting, protecting, and educating about intellectual freedom. It serves as a point of voluntary access to information and ideas and as a learning laboratory for students as they acquire critical thinking and problem-solving skills needed in a pluralistic society. . . . Under these principles, all students have equitable access to library facilities, resources, and instructional programs.
>
> School librarians assume a leadership role in promoting the principles of intellectual freedom . . . .
>
> School librarians resist efforts by individuals or groups to define what is appropriate for all students or teachers to read, view, hear, or access regardless of technology, formats or method of delivery.
>
> Major barriers between students and resources include but are not limited to: imposing age, grade-level, or reading-level restrictions on the use of resources; limiting the use of interlibrary loan and access to electronic information; charging fees for information in specific formats; requiring permission from parents or teachers; establishing restricted shelves or closed collections; and labeling. (ALA 2014a)

AN ELEMENTARY SCHOOL LIBRARIAN'S EXEMPLAR

As your school librarian, I promise to:

» Provide you with lots of books you will love to read both for pleasure and for information.
» Help you find the book that is just right for you.
» Teach you how to find what you need.
» Allow you to make your own choices.
» Protect your right to privacy.
» Trust you to take care of your books and return them when you are finished.
» Give you the time to explore what your school library has to offer.
» Furnish you with a comfy place to curl up with a good book.
» Defend you against censorship.

—Christine Carey, School Librarian, Bushy Park Elementary School, Howard County Public Schools, Maryland

What Is Intellectual Freedom?

ALA's definition of intellectual freedom is short and to the point. You may want to post this definition, especially if you are a middle or high school librarian.

> Intellectual freedom is the right of every individual to both seek and receive information from all points of view without restriction. It provides for free access to all expressions of ideas through which any and all sides of a question, cause, or movement may be explored. (ALA 2007)

Coping with Challenges

The ALA "Coping with Challenges" document helps school librarians because it addresses ways to work with children. The statement begins with the heading "Kids and Libraries: What You Should Know" and then goes on to answer six key questions. Following are key points to remember.

How do librarians select their collections?
Because an item is selected does not mean the librarian endorses or promotes it. He or she is simply helping the library to fulfill its mission of providing information from all points of view.

Can't parents tell the librarian what material they don't think children should have?
Decisions about what materials are suitable for particular children should be made by the people who know them best—their parents or guardians. . . .

It is the right and responsibility of parents to guide their own family's library use while allowing other parents to do the same.

Librarians are not authorized to act as parents. But they are happy to provide suggestions and guidance to parents and youngsters at any time. (ALA 1999)

Labeling Books with Reading Levels

Let's be clear. Don't post reading levels on books. And, do not restrict young learners to certain sections of the school library. See the sections on labeling and restricting access in the ALA document *Labeling Systems: An Interpretation of the Library Bill of Rights*. Books should not be labeled with Lexile reading levels, as young learners deserve privacy on their reading abilities.

The AASL Position Statement on Labeling Books with Reading Levels was first published in 2011 in response to educators asking school librarians to label books with Lexile reading levels. This statement is marked for review and revision again in 2019 to align with the *National School Library Standards*.

Using reading levels works in the language arts classroom but not in the school library. Of course, you should teach young learners the five-finger rule—if a page has five words the learner doesn't know, then the book *might* be too hard—but make this rule a suggestion, *not* a requirement. Besides, there is no rule demanding that learners read every single word in a book. Do you read every word?

Likewise, genrefying a collection may not be a wise idea. You must teach learners how to locate materials in your school library, so they can then locate materials in *all* libraries. What you determine and label as a mystery might be classified as fantasy by someone else.

I've known elementary school librarians who restrict the primary learners to the "Everybody" section. Or the school librarian will display preselected titles on the tables and insist the youngest learners select from those. I've known middle school librarians who keep a section restricted for the eighth graders. Maybe the school librarians' intentions are good, but these practices are just plain wrong.

Learners need to feel trusted to make wise decisions, and they need plenty of practice in independently selecting what they need. That's why you allow learners to come in daily and check out books.

> Labeling Systems: The American Library Association affirms the rights of individuals to form their own opinions about resources they choose to read, view, listen to, or otherwise access . . . Labeling systems present distinct challenges to these intellectual freedom principles. (ALA 2015)

> Restricted Access to Library Materials: Libraries are a traditional forum for the open exchange of information. Attempts to restrict access to library materials violate the basic tenets of the Library Bill of Rights. (ALA 2014)

Library Privacy Guidelines for Students in K–12 Schools

I'm sorry to say I didn't respect the privacy of my learners. I pasted overdue lists all over the school. I read aloud learners' names and the books they had checked out. Agh! Don't make my mistake. Read this key information.

> Students' and minors' First Amendment rights to free inquiry and privacy must be balanced against both the educational needs of the school and the rights of the parents. As students and minors mature, it is increasingly important that they are provided with opportunities to exercise their curiosity and develop their intellect free from the chilling effects of surveillance by educators, peers, parents, or commercial interests. As students begin to participate more fully in the online world, they must develop an appreciation for their own privacy and a corresponding respect for the privacy of others. (ALA 2016)

YOUR TURN

Chapter 7—How Do I Turn a Complaint into a Positive?

In this chapter, what were the most important ideas that surprised or resonated with you?

_____

_____

_____

_____

List the documents you will share with your learners. What are the ways you will share this knowledge?

_____

_____

_____

_____

Restate these documents in your own words in a way that your learners will understand.

_____

_____

_____

_____

Chapter 7 worksheet supporting *An Introduction to Collection Development for School Librarians* by Mona Kerby, © 2019 American Library Association.

 For a one-page, printable version of this worksheet, go to **alaeditions.org/webextras.**

How Do I Showcase the Collection?

Ah, we come back to the rewarding objective of our school librarian profession—to not only build the collection but also ensure that the collection is *used.* So how exactly do you showcase a collection?

AASL is ready to the rescue. The *National School Library Standards* provide guidance. The AASL Standards web portal provides many helpful resources. An entire book could be devoted to implementation strategies for showcasing our collections and our services. In short, our task boils down to two short words: *share* and *communicate.*

In figure 8.1, I've selected five School Library Domains and Alignments that pertain to showcasing the collection (AASL 2018, 84–105). Again, the most important ideas are in boldface.

The standards also identify ten best practices on curation. These three are essential for showcasing your collection:

- Ensure that your online catalog and digital resources are available 24/7.
- Create and share self-guided instructions on resources.
- Teach digital tools, including tools in curation and in citation. (AASL 2018, 101–102)

If you are in graduate school, you will likely have an assignment to meet the ALA/AASL/CAEP Component 5.3 Advocacy whereby you advocate for learners, resources, and school libraries.

FIGURE 8.1

National School Library Standards: School Library Domains
and Alignments for Showcasing the Collection

Shared Foundations	School Library Domains and Alignments
III. Collaborate	**C. SHARE:** The school library provides opportunities for school librarians to connect and work with the learning community by: • III.C.2. Designing and **leading professional-development** opportunities that **reinforce the impact of the school library's resources, services, and programming** on learners' academic learning and educators' effectiveness. • III.C.3. Promoting and modeling the importance of information-use skills by **publicizing** to learners, staff, and the community available **services and resources;** serving on school and district-wide committees; and engaging in community and professional activities.
IV. Curate	**C. SHARE:** The school library facilitates the contribution and exchange of information within and among learning communities by: • IV.C.2. Including and tracking collection materials in **a system that uses standardized approaches to description and location.** • IV.C.3. Establishing policies that promote effective acquisition, description, circulation, sharing, and **access to resources within and beyond the school day.**
V. Explore	**C. SHARE:** The school library prepares learners to engage with a larger learning community by: • V.C.2. **Encouraging families** and other members of the community **to participate in school library activities.** • V.C.3. Building and **advocating** for strong relationships with stakeholders who recognize and support an **effective school library**.
VI. Engage	**C. SHARE:** The school library encourages participation in a diverse learning community to create and share information by: • VI.C.2. Providing a context in which the school librarian can model for learners, other educators, and administrators **multiple strategies to locate, evaluate, and ethically use information** for specific purposes.

Source: Excerpted from the AASL *National School Library Standards for Learners, School Librarians, and School Libraries*, standards.aasl.org, © 2018 American Library Association.

ADVOCACY

We have a district-level school library association, and I am an elementary representative. We advocate for school libraries in the school and greater community. We share how school librarians prepare learners to be college or career ready.

—Dina Kropkowski, School Librarian, Forest Lakes Elementary School, Harford County Public Schools, Maryland

Establishing Digital Access 24/7

Alignment IV.C.3. in the School Library framework states that we promote circulation of and access to resources within and beyond the school day. That means you need a dynamic school library website with 24/7 access. The district is likely to have restrictions on website development, but don't let the frustrations stop you from providing a rich access to resources.

Creating Pathfinders

Alignment VI.C.2. in the School Library framework reminds us that we model and provide "multiple strategies to locate, evaluate, and ethically use information for specific purposes." Pathfinders help learners meet this Alignment. Split up the work with other school librarians or have learners create pathfinders because they will need the experience in curation. Although you can purchase software such as LibGuides or LiveBinders, you might have just as much success by crafting your own.

Template for Creating Pathfinders

Design a pleasing page layout that is professional and attractive and that aids in reader understanding. The following are suggested headings.

Title, purpose, scope, grade level—Briefly title the pathfinder so the objective is obvious. Write a short sentence that identifies the educator, grade level, and classroom subject for which the pathfinder is to be used.

- *Library books*—Include Dewey call numbers, subject headings, and sample search terms. You might also list the best book titles. Provide a link to the library catalog.

- *Online databases*—List and link to the relevant databases. Include search instructions, if needed.
- *Image resources*—Provide a direct link to images that support this subject.
- *Specific websites*—Identify only the best. Provide links and brief annotations. If there are many websites, consider arranging them in categories.
- *Video resources*—Provide a direct link to video resources that support this subject.
- *Citation information*—Provide links to citation tools so learners correctly cite resources.
- *Additional categories*—Use this heading if you have additional resources to share.
- *Signature and date*—Always date your work; you'll be revising the pathfinder and having the current date ensures that learners are using the latest and most accurate resources.

Teaching Digital Tools

Implementing Alignment IV.C.2. can be helpful when later teaching learners to curate sources for themselves. Learner curation can be aided by using digital tools and is an easy way to meet Alignment VI.D.2. in the School Library framework whereby you engage learners with innovative information technologies. Each year AASL announces the latest lists of Best Apps for Teaching & Learning and Best Websites for Teaching & Learning and also shares instructional and promotional materials for these lists.

DATA SHARKS

"This librarian takes responsibility/blame for any kid who manages to graduate from school without being a first-rate data shark."

—Seth Godin (2011), American author, business executive, and blogger

Leadership, Advocacy, and Communication

Showcasing the collection depends on your successful ability to lead, advocate, and communicate.

Alignment III.C.3. charges school librarians with "promoting and modeling the importance of information-use skills by publicizing to learners, staff, and the community available services and resources; serving on school and district-wide committees; and engaging in community and professional activities." This leadership might include strategies such as communicating to parents through the school library website, at PTA events, and at library-sponsored events; using Twitter and book displays; displaying student learner projects; and having student learners make morning announcements (AASL 2015, 5–6).

"Building and advocating for strong relationships with stakeholders who recognize and support an effective school library" is essential (AASL 2018, School Library V.C.3.). As an advocate, you might be partnering with the PTA to fund-raise for library materials and networking with public librarians by notifying them of upcoming research projects and by helping learners obtain public library cards (AASL 2015, 11–17).

As a communicator, encourage "families and other members of the community to participate in school library activities" (AASL 2018, School Library V.C.2.) by developing a monthly "what's happening in the school library" e-newsletter to showcase the ways you and your program impact learning; creating an archive of "tech tips" on the school library website and adding tips frequently; providing a Tech Tip of the Week/Month; and archiving copies of your newsletters, annual reports, and promotional flyers on the website. Other suggestions include creating (or asking student learners to create) "how-to" screencasts on any program or action that you have had to explain more than once; having student learners send home an e-mail about the technology and inquiry-based projects they are working on in the school library; taking pictures that the learners can attach to their messages home; and offering coding classes or makerspace afterschool programs in the school library (AASL 2015, 25–33).

"Designing and leading professional-development opportunities that reinforce the impact of the school library's resources, services, and programming on learners' academic learning and educators' effectiveness" can also be a powerful communication and advocacy strategy for showcasing the resources and services you provide (AASL 2018, School Library III.C.2.). Consider developing a recurring professional development night during which you can showcase new resources and tech tools, and educators can explore, tinker, and use that time to network and begin creating something to use with their learners.

WAYS I COMMUNICATE

» I have a school library blog with pages for our class schedule, hours, policies, and information about our programs, such as Battle of the Books, One School One Book, and Family Reading Night. The main page shares upcoming events, reminders, and photos. Learners and families write comments and ask questions.

» I offer monthly after-school professional development. This year, it's Tech Thursdays where I highlight databases and new tools, such as AASL Best Apps. I allow time for educators to use the tool to begin creating something for their classes.

» On every worksheet, I include a header that says "School Library Activity" or "Today in the School Library, we . . . ." This simple strategy lets parents know what we are learning.

—Jamie Rooney, School Librarian, Ebb Valley Elementary School,
Carroll County Public Schools, Maryland

Celebrating events such as School Library Month, National Library Week, Chemistry Month, or Be Kind to Pets Week is a great way to meet Alignment V.C.2. Many of these observances come "ready-made" with publicity materials and activities. Other events to celebrate include the following:

- February: Library Lovers' Month
- March: Digital Learning Day
- April: El día de los niños/El día de los libros, Poetry Month, and D.E.A.R—Drop Everything and Read Day
- May: Get Caught Reading Month
- June: GLBT Book Month
- September: Banned Books Week and International Literacy Day
- October: Teen Read Week
- November: Picture Book Month
- December: Hour of Code (AASL 2015, 38, 43–44, 59–65)

To an extent, showcasing the collection is just smart advertisement—celebrating holidays, having morning announcements, sending newsletters. But successful advertisement is only a surface-level accomplishment. You're doing something much more powerful. Through leadership, you are uniting the community into seeking this dynamic goal—using the school library to improve the intellectual and emotional lives of all learners—forever.

YOUR TURN

Chapter 8—How Do I Showcase the Collection?

In this chapter, what were the most important ideas that surprised or resonated with you?

_____

_____

_____

_____

List the pathfinders and sets of online instructions you need to write. Identify the school librarians and student learners who will help with the work, and set a time line.

_____

_____

_____

_____

Select three additional ways to showcase your collection, and list your steps in accomplishing them.

_____

_____

_____

_____

Chapter 8 worksheet supporting *An Introduction to Collection Development for School Librarians* by Mona Kerby, © 2019 American Library Association.

 For a one-page, printable version of this worksheet, go to **alaeditions.org/webextras.**

AFTERWORD
Cheering You Onward!

It has been a rainy, dreary few weeks in Maryland. Folks in North Carolina are coping with the lingering effects of Hurricane Florence. But on this Friday afternoon as I sit at my desk finishing this book, the sun is shining.

Even though your school librarian career will be different than mine, some things remain the same. In 1931 S. A. Ranganathan wrote the Five Laws of Library Science, but even today, the simplicity of the statement captures what librarians do.

1. Books are for use.
2. Every reader his book.
3. Every book its reader.
4. Save the time of the reader.
5. A library is a growing organism. (Ranganathan, 1931)

In 1978 Sue Rose, the school library director for the Arlington (Texas) Independent School District, hired me as one of the first of six elementary school librarians in our district. I had not taken a single library course, but in that interview, I said I wanted to teach every child in the building. Sue Rose was looking for library-teachers. I got the job.

In 2018 AASL published the most forward-thinking standards we've ever had. But our mission remains constant. School libraries meet the needs of *all* learners. School library collections are for *use*. School librarians are *educators*.

How fortunate we are to have such important careers—changing the lives of learners, teaching them to be thriving digital citizens, always sharing our love of reading.

Sue Rose changed my life. I learned how to be a school librarian by copying Sue. She died last week. This book is my attempt to help you, to "pay forward" what she gave to me.

Think of me as your cheerleader. You can do this fun and rewarding job. Onward!

—Mona Kerby

BIBLIOGRAPHY

Note: Abbreviations are used for American Library Association (ALA), American Association of School Librarians (AASL), Association for Library Service to Children (ALSC), and Young Adult Library Services Association (YALSA).

AASL. 2011. "Position Statement on Labeling Books with Reading Levels." www.ala.org/aasl/advocacy/resources/statements/labeling.

AASL. 2015. "Toolkit for Promoting School Library Programs: Messages, Ideas, and Strategies for Communicating the Value of School Library Programs and School Librarians in the 21st Century." www.ala.org/aasl/sites/ala.org.aasl/files/content/aaslissues/toolkits/promo/AASL_Toolkit_Promoting_SLP_033016.pdf.

AASL. 2018. *National School Library Standards for Learners, School Librarians, and School Libraries.* ALA: Chicago.

AASL. "Best Apps for Teaching & Learning." www.ala.org/aasl/standards/best/apps.

AASL. "Best Websites for Teaching & Learning." www.ala.org/aasl/standards/best/websites.

ALA. 1996. "Library Bill of Rights." Last modified January 29, 2019. www.ala.org/advocacy/intfreedom/librarybill.

ALA. 1999. "Coping with Challenges. Kids and Libraries: What You Should Know." www.ala.org/advocacy/bbooks/challengedmaterials/preparation/coping.

ALA. 2004. "The Freedom to Read Statement." Last modified June 30, 2004. www.ala.org/advocacy/intfreedom/freedomreadstatement.

ALA. 2007. "Intellectual Freedom and Censorship Q & A." Last modified May 29, 2007. www.ala.org/advocacy/intfreedom/censorship/faq.

ALA. 2008. "Professional Ethics." Last modified January 22, 2008. www.ala.org/tools/ethics.

ALA. 2014a. *Access to Resources and Services in the School Library: An Interpretation of the Library Bill of Rights.* www.ala.org/advocacy/intfreedom/librarybill/interpretations/accessresources.

ALA. 2014b. Restricted Access to Library Materials: An Interpretation of the Library Bill of Rights. www.ala.org/advocacy/intfreedom/librarybill/interpretations/restrictedaccess.

ALA. 2015. Labeling Systems: An Interpretation of the Library Bill of Rights. www.ala.org/advocacy/intfreedom/librarybill/interpretation/labeling-systems.

ALA. 2016. "Library Privacy Guidelines for Students in K–12 Schools." http://www.ala.org/advocacy/privacy/guidelines/students.

ALA. 2018. "Selection & Reconsideration Policy Toolkit for Public, School, & Academic Libraries." http://www.ala.org/tools/challengesupport/selectionpolicytoolkit.

ALA/AASL/CAEP. Forthcoming. *ALA/AASL/CAEP Standards for Initial Preparation of School Librarians.* Approved by Specialty Areas Studies Board (SASB) of the Council for the Accreditation of Educator Preparation.

ALA/Ethnic & Multicultural Information Exchange Round Table. "The Coretta Scott King Book Award." www.ala.org/rt/emiert/cskbookawards.

ALA/Feminist Task Force of the Social Responsibilities Round Table. "The Amelia Bloomer Book List." www.ala.org/awardsgrants/amelia-bloomer-book-list.

ALA/Gay, Lesbian, Bisexual, and Transgender Round Table. "Rainbow Book List." https://glbtrt.ala.org/rainbowbooks/archives/1270.

ALA/Gay, Lesbian, Bisexual, and Transgender Round Table. "Stonewall Book Award." www.ala.org/rt/glbtrt/award/stonewall.

ALA. "Schneider Family Book Award." www.ala.org/awardsgrants/schneider-family-book-award.

ALSC. "Book & Media Awards." www.ala.org/alsc/awardsgrants/bookmedia.

ALSC. "Children's Notable Lists." www.ala.org/alsc/awardsgrants/notalists.

ALSC. "Robert F. Sibert Informational Book Medal." http://www.ala.org/alsc/awardsgrants/bookmedia/sibertmedal.

Association of University Presses. "University Press Books for Public and Secondary School Libraries." http://aupresses.org/news-a-publications/aaup-publications/university-press-books-for-libraries.

Booklist. https://www.booklistonline.com.

Children's Literature & Reading Special Interest Group, International Literacy Association. "Notable Books for a Global Society." https://www.clrsig.org/notable-books-for-a-global-society-nbgs.html.

Common Sense Media. https://www.commonsensemedia.org.

Godin, Seth. 2011. "The Future of the Library." *Seth's Blog.* May 16. http://sethgodin.typepad.com/seths_blog/2011/05/the-future-of-the-library.html%20.

Grey House Publishing. H. W. Wilson Core Collections. https://www.hwwilsoninprint.com/core_collections.php.

Horn Book Guide. https://www.hbook.com/horn-book-guide/.

International Literacy Association. "Children's Choices Reading List." https://www.literacyworldwide.org/docs/default-source/reading-lists/childrens-choices/childrens-choices-reading-list-2018.pdf.

Kirkus. https://www.kirkusreviews.com.

Larson, J., & Texas State Library and Archives Commission. 2012. "CREW: A Weeding Manual for Modern Libraries." https://www.tsl.texas.gov/sites/default/files/public/tslac/ld/ld/pubs/crew/crewmethod12.pdf.

Maryland Association of School Librarians. "Maryland Black-Eyed Susan Book Award." http://maslmd.org/about-bes/.

National Council for the Social Studies. "Notable Social Studies Trade Books for Young People." https://www.socialstudies.org/publications/notables.

National Science Teachers Association. "Best STEM Books K–12." https://www.nsta.org/publications/stembooks/.

National Science Teachers Association. "Outstanding Science Trade Books for Students K–12." https://www.nsta.org/publications/ostb/.

Pennsylvania School Librarians Association. "Pennsylvania Young Reader's Choice Awards Program." https://www.psla.org/pennsylvania-young-reader-s-choice-awards-program.

Ranganathan, S. A. 1931. "Five Laws of Library Science . . . Detailing the Principles of Operating a Library System." http://aims.fao.org/activity/blog/five-laws-library-science-detailing-principles-operating-library-system.

School Library Journal. https://www.slj.com.

Smith, Cynthia Leitich: Official Author Site and Home of Children's and YA Lit Resources. (n.d.). "Awards for Children's and YA Literature by State." https://cynthialeitichsmith.com/lit-resources/read/awards/stateawards/.

Texas Library Association. "Texas Bluebonnet Award." https://txla.org/tools-resources/reading-lists/texas-bluebonnet-award/about/.

United States Board on Books for Young People (USBBY). "Outstanding International Books List." https://www.usbby.org/outstanding-international-books-list.html.

VOYA Magazine. http://voyamagazine.com/tags/book-reviews/.

We Need Diverse Books. https://diversebooks.org.

YALSA. "YALSA Book and Media Awards for Libraries." www.ala.org/yalsa/bookawards/booklists/members.

INDEX

www.ingramcontent.com/pod-product-compliance
Lightning Source LLC
Jackson TN
JSHW060856070125
76677JS00002B/4